The Practical Guide to

Debating

Worlds Style/
British Parliamentary Style

The Practical Guide to

Debating

Worlds Style/
British Parliamentary Style

Neill Harvey-Smith

International Debate Education Association
New York, London & Amsterdam

Published by:
International Debate Education Association
400 West 59th Street
New York, NY 10019

Library of Congress Cataloging-in-Publication Data

Harvey-Smith, Neill.
    The practical guide to debating, worlds style/British parliamentary style/
Neill Harvey-Smith.
        p.   cm.
    ISBN 978-1-61770-016-3
1. Parliamentary practice—Handbooks, manuals, etc.   2. Debates and
debating—Handbooks, manuals, etc.   3. Parliamentary practice—
Competitions—Handbooks, manuals, etc.   4. Debates and debating—
Competitions—Handbooks, manuals, etc.   I. Title.
    JF515.H245 2011
    808.53—dc22   2011015918

Design by Brad Walrod/Kenoza Type
Printed in the USA

IDEBATE Press

To Beth, whose love makes all things possible, and Rosie, who interrupted and inspired in equal measures

Contents

3 How to Adjudicate   *67*

Introduction

Debate

People have always argued. From the ancient polis to the modern pub, differences of opinion have been a central part of how men and women define themselves and interact with others. Whether for self-expression in the social arena or as the prelude to a duel, words have always had bite. They can resolve disagreements and they can accentuate them.

Debate is a particular form of argument. It is not a way of reconciling differences—that is a misconception. Debate is a way of arbitrating between differences. The purpose of a debate is not for two disputing parties to leave the room in agreement. Instead, through the debate between them, others will form a judgment about which of the two to support.

Debate recognizes that people are capable of disagreeing on everything about which it is possible to hold an opinion. It relishes those conflicts and provides a means by which to agree on common action. While the contrasts are often extreme and the language forceful, the process is consensual and peaceful.

Debate is, by its nature, a formal activity. It is the act of a third party deciding between the two sides that distinguishes debate from any other verbal fight. To form that judgment, the listening audience requires the protagonists to follow certain rules and protocols.

So, having a debate is distinct from having an argument. In an argument, your target is your interlocutor, whose mind you wish to change. In a debate, while you do argue with fellow debaters, your target is the adjudication panel.

A debate also differs from a public speaking competition. In public speaking, an individual tries to move an audience with the power of her oratory. This is part of debating—but only a part. A debate witnesses a progression of ideas, with each speaker having an important role to play in ensuring that the subject under discussion gets full and deep analysis.

Worlds Style

The form of debate this book discusses is Worlds Style (WS) debating, currently the most popular, most international and fastest-growing format of competitive debate. It is the format used in the World Universities' Debating Championships (known informally as Worlds) and underpins hundreds of other competitions every year, so by learning it, you can enter a global debate community.

What I refer to throughout this book as Worlds Style is normally termed British Parliamentary (BP) debate, which grew out of the traditions of the United Kingdom Parliament in Westminster and follows some of the conventions of the House of Commons. A Government and Opposition face each other. The order of speeches crosses the house, alternating between each side. There are Points of Information, similar to the interventions that members of Parliament permit each other to make. The motion is worded "This House" and treated like a bill that will either pass into law or fail. In 1994, the World Universities' Debating Council decided to adopt

British Parliamentary as the style for all future World Championships. This decision led, eventually, to the growth of WS debate worldwide.

Over the last decades, British Parliamentary style has changed dramatically. In the mid-nineties, intervarsity debating competitions in BP style predominantly had five-minute speeches, open motions (broad, ambiguously worded motions that could apply to a wide range of topics—for example, "This House Would Rather Be Shaken Than Stirred"), judging based greatly on manner, no adjudicator feedback, black-tie finals, and a pervasive culture of heavy drinking.

None of this would be recognizable to most debaters of the present day. The form of debate codified for Worlds has clearly defined motions, seven-minute speeches, and feedback after the first seven rounds. It has a stable set of rules that have remained unaltered for well over a decade, giving an amazing continuity of learning materials and adjudication expertise that make it especially rewarding. With long-standing rules and structures to level the playing field between debaters, Worlds Style is highly suitable for speakers of English as a second language whatever their level of English proficiency.

Worlds Style is both a sport, with competitions taking place all over the world, and retains something of the art of debate, with manner—style and structure—given consideration alongside matter.

As Worlds has grown, so the rules of debating have standardized. Debaters have increasingly chosen to attend tournaments that will prepare them for the pinnacle of competition. These tournaments are more international and yet more homogeneous. Standardization has extended to adjudication. Matter and volume of argumentation have counted for more as the years have passed. Assessing manner has been treated with suspicion by some, partly out of a positive desire to avoid discrimination against speakers whose first language is not English.

Rules only tell you so much about the real experience of debating in Worlds Style, however. You are reading a practical guide that aims to help you debate now. In the following pages, I will share the conventions of modern Worlds Style debate.

The Growth of Worlds Style

In its early days, international debating was largely confined to what Winston Churchill called the "English-speaking peoples." When the World Championships began in 1981, there were 43 teams from seven countries taking part: England, Scotland, Ireland, United States, Canada, New Zealand, and Australia. Now, more than four hundred teams from 60 countries participate; the most recent hosts have been Botswana, Turkey, Ireland, Thailand, Canada, and Malaysia.

Worlds Style debate is used for major international tournaments. Besides Worlds, competitions with global reach are held in Malaysia, the United Kingdom, and the United States. North America, Africa, the Middle East, Europe, Asia, and Australasia host regional championships.

Where once WS was synonymous with British debating, it now spans Europe and has extended throughout the globe. Teams and tournaments can now be found in Austria, Finland, the Netherlands, Croatia, Israel, Russia, Latvia, Estonia, Lithuania, France, Germany, Greece, Serbia, Ukraine, Slovenia, Sweden, Switzerland, Romania, Poland, Kazakhstan, Turkey, the Czech Republic, France, Ukraine, Montenegro, and Macedonia. In Asia, WS debate is big in China, Japan, Mongolia, Hong Kong, Republic of Korea, Taiwan, Macau, Singapore, Thailand, Malaysia, India, Sri Lanka, Bangladesh, Pakistan, Indonesia, and the Philippines. The first Middle East Debate Academy, held in 2010, invited debaters from Iraq, Qatar, Azerbaijan, Oman, Iran, Saudi Arabia, and Turkey. WS debate in Africa extends to Nigeria, Ghana, Uganda, Kenya, Botswana, Lesotho, Zambia, Namibia, Zimbabwe, South Africa, Liberia, Tanzania,

Angola, Malawi, and Swaziland. In the Caribbean and Latin America, WS debates and debaters can be found in Barbados, Trinidad and Tobago, Jamaica, Peru, and Venezuela.

Online debate is also growing, with a World Online Debating Championships involving debaters from every continent held annually in WS.

The Power of Worlds Style

With its international reach, Worlds Style offers wonderful opportunities to deepen cultural awareness, knowledge, and understanding. Debaters can travel the world, interacting under a set of common rules, discussing topics of interest to local people. Debating ASEAN reform in Indonesia or whaling in Japan are broadening experiences. WS opens doors to a global community of people committed to discussing ideas and to debating openly and fairly.

WS debate promotes a willingness to engage outside of a debater's specific point of view. Speakers are assigned to one side of a motion at random, not according to their beliefs. They must, therefore, be able to speak persuasively regardless of their personal feelings on a matter. Assigning positions provides systemic incentives to engage with, understand, and articulate the widest possible breadth of positions. Not only does WS furnish speakers with a range of alternatives against which to compare their own opinions, it develops and eventually embeds an analytical thought process that compels them to think critically about those beliefs.

Flexibility and mental dexterity are required to engage with the arguments and evidence presented by others. Debating is a largely spontaneous activity, with only 15 minutes' preparation time the norm. Successful debaters require deep understanding of a range of positions, command of nuance, and an intuitive sense of connections between ideas. They are rewarded for taking opposing arguments at their strongest, not their weakest. Caricature, superficial rejection, or wholesale dismissal of a well-argued case are penalized in debate. Anticipating and engaging with a multiplicity of views are required. Speakers who reduce issues to two simple sides or just parrot lists of pros and cons will not excel.

Speakers need to think broadly and subtly—they are expected to encourage people holding a range of viewpoints to come together in support of an action. Taking just one opinion and repeating it brings less success than showing why people of different views can find reasons to agree with you. "So, you don't agree war is never justified? I'll show you why it cannot be justified in this instance."

The multiplicity of views considered must include international perspectives. WS debates generally take place in an undefined world forum, international body, or "liberal democracies." Adjudicators and other teams are often from different political systems and cultures. Engaging with them requires finding common ground. The easy legal argument that a particular policy violates the U.S. Constitution is not compelling in an international forum.

Whatever the subject, the critical-thinking skills and deliberative process inherent in debate are valuable for learning and personal growth. That is why, contrary to myth, the world's finest debaters are not only lawyers and political science students, but medical students, astrophysicists, historians, economists, linguists, and computer scientists.

1

Getting Started

In life, many of us have a tendency to avoid doing something publicly until we are satisfied that we are really good at it. When learning another language, we can be reluctant to speak until our accent is just right. Giving a presentation, we want every word written down just in case we forget.

Debate is something you learn by doing. There are a thousand resources and rules that you could read before standing up and speaking for the first time. Ignore them—they will overload you. The first step to debating well is becoming confident at standing up and speaking in public.

The prime necessity is people. Initially, you need enough people to have two sides and an audience. That could be no more than three people! One person in favor, one against, and one person deciding who was more persuasive.

Then your club will grow. So long as you have the same number of speakers on each side, you can have 1 v 1, 2 v 2, 3 v 3, or 4 v 4, with the people left over judging the debate. Divide a group of eight into two teams of three, with two judges—alternate the speeches between Government and Opposition, then allow the judges to decide who won.

As numbers rise further, you can have 4 v 4 debates, then allow audience members to make floor speeches after the main debate (speeches in the main debate are called platform speeches). A floor speech is a chance to make a short contribution, perhaps only 30 seconds, and a great way to get a nervous new club member to make his first speech. At the first debate I attended, in the grand Council Chamber of the University of Leeds, I was extremely nervous but managed to think of three lines to say and made a very short floor speech at the end of the evening. People clapped, I felt better about myself, and two weeks later had enough confidence to accept an invitation to make a platform speech.

As numbers grow, you can make the debates more formal. Appoint a Speaker, whose job it is to call each of the participants when it is time to speak. Have a timekeeper, ensuring the speeches are all the same length—perhaps only three, four, or five minutes when your club is new.

It is important to give everyone a chance to experience all the different roles in debate: speaking in Government, in Opposition, adjudicating, acting as Speaker, and timekeeping. By seeing debates from all angles, you gain a sense of what is happening and a deeper understanding of how it all works.

Once you have people, all you need is a little bit of knowledge and a lot of positive attitude. The basic skills can be learned quickest if you are open, welcoming, and create a space where people feel happy to fail in the pursuit of success.

Basic Skills

The wrong way to learn how to debate is to write a speech in full and then read it out. The right way can be summarized as SALSA:

Speaking—talking out loud fluently and without hesitation
Arguing—condensing what you say into a persuasive point(s)
Listening—hearing and understanding the points others make
Synthesizing—matching the points you and others make
Arranging—structuring your points into a persuasive speech

Start with just talking. Tell the group the best or worst thing that happened this week. Do it without notes and try to make it engaging. Get comfortable just telling a story and having others listen to you. Easy, comfortable delivery without notes is what you need to take into your debating.

Once you feel comfortable, move on to drills, games, and activities that get you practicing arguing, listening, synthesizing, and arranging. Here are four suggestions to get you going.

1. Switch

Form a circle. One person announces the motion—assisted suicide should be legalized, for example—then points to another person and says "switch," whereupon that second person has to start speaking, making an argument in favor of the motion. A switch happens every 30 seconds in the same way, with each new speaker continuing as if it were the same speech.

After a while, the group leader says "change" and people have to start making arguments against the motion, switching between speakers as before.

Excellent listening skills are needed to follow the thread of an argument and be able to continue it without pause; disciplined arguing skills are another necessity if you are going to make a point in just 30 seconds; and synthesizing skills are required to flip between reasons to support/oppose the motion off the top of your head.

2. Bluff

Everybody writes a question on a piece of paper—a debatable and difficult question—something to which the person writing does not know the answer. Examples might include: "How should we solve the problem of deforestation in South America?" or "Should there be a salary cap on soccer players in Japan?" The papers are folded and put in a bowl. Each person picks a question, reads it, and gives a clear, fluent, and persuasive one-minute answer. This may be your opinion, you may have genuine evidence to back it up—or you may not. The purpose here is not to discover the "truth" but to develop confidence in persuasion. If you can speak well on a topic about which you know little, with no preparation time, it will boost your ability to cope with any situation you encounter in a debate.

Bluff is a great way to practice speaking and arguing.

3. Change the World

If standing up in front of an audience makes you nervous, Change the World is an exercise that can help. Come up with one idea that you think would make the world a better place. Then sell your idea to the group. You need to explain the idea and be passionate about its benefits. With no time limit, this is a chance to stand up, talk, and sound like you mean it. To make it competitive, group members can vote on the best idea at the end. Change the World is primarily a speaking and arguing exercise. But if debaters must say why their idea is better than those proposed by others, it can also be a listening and synthesizing exercise.

4. Balloon Debate

A great activity based on a peculiar premise—you are a famous person of your choice in a hot air balloon hurtling toward the earth. It cannot take the weight of everyone, and some passengers must be thrown overboard to save the rest (the group decides the number!). You must make a passionate case for keeping you on board the balloon. The strangeness of the scenario allows people to relax and be passionate in their public speaking. This is a great exercise to develop speaking and arguing skills; as the appeals to throw someone else overboard begin, you start to see listening and synthesizing, too.

Experience Debates

Whenever you get the chance to speak, take it. If your club allows floor speeches, make a contribution, however short. If you have a training session, volunteer even if the subject is not one of your favorites.

If that isn't possible, remember that you don't have to speak in a debate to learn about debating. When you hear other speakers, reflect on what they are saying, enjoy the experience of having them try to persuade you, and consider what works for you.

Ensure that everyone in your club, however inexperienced, gets a chance to adjudicate debates. If you haven't been asked, volunteer! Listening, weighing the issues, and engaging with experienced judges—a great way to learn.

Read a quality newspaper or news website every day to get a handle on global issues. Debate motions can be about anything from politics and economics to culture and sports. Don't just mine news sources for information, but think critically about the issues and the different viewpoints involved. As your awareness grows, you will start to make connections and see subtle distinctions within a whole range of events.

If you can't get to attend live debates by experienced debaters, then use the Internet. Look up debates on Google and YouTube—WUDC is the usual abbreviation for Worlds—and see how champion debaters operate. By no means copy them, but watch and see how persuasive you find them. Consider adopting those techniques that you like and admire into your own style, but make sure you keep your own authentic voice.

Formal Debate—Mechanics and Language

Eventually, you need to participate in a formal debate. Here are some basic WS rules and conventions you need to know. One of the strengths of WS debate is that it involves few formalities. Keeping them in mind, watch a debate online—you should easily be able to follow what is going on. Then try it for yourself.

A debate has a *motion*—the topic to be discussed. It takes the form "This House..." and determines the course of action that is to be proposed. For example:

> This House Would Bring Home All UN Peacekeepers from Sierra Leone
> This House Would Boycott the Olympics
> This House Would Allow Wiretap Evidence to Be Used in Court

Sometimes a motion will read "This House Believes..." For example:

> This House Believes Chechnya Has a Right to Independence
> This House Believes in a Woman's Right to Choose

Regardless of the variation in wording, the job of the first Government speaker is to propose and explain a course of action. For example, in the last two examples, the first Government speaker would be expected, in the first, to suggest a course of action that would secure Chechen independence and, in the second, ensuring that the law protected a woman's right to choose an abortion.

The two sides in the debate are Government and Opposition, each of which is represented by two teams. The four teams (of two speakers) are called Opening Government, Closing Government, Opening Opposition, and Closing Opposition. Government and Opposition are called the two sides of the House or just the two sides. Each team's position in the debate is drawn at random just before the debate begins. They have 15 minutes to prepare; in this time, they decide which team member speaks first and which second.

The order of speakers is as follows:

> Opening Government (first speaker) or Prime Minister
> Opening Opposition (first speaker) or Leader of the Opposition

Opening Government (second speaker) or Deputy Prime Minister

Opening Opposition (second speaker) or Deputy Leader of the Opposition

Closing Government (first speaker) or Member for the Government

Closing Opposition (first speaker) or Member for the Opposition

Closing Government (second speaker) or Government Whip

Closing Opposition (second speaker) or Opposition Whip

OPENING GOVERNMENT	OPENING OPPOSITION
1. Prime Minister	2. Leader of the Opposition
3. Deputy Prime Minister	4. Deputy Leader of the Opposition
CLOSING GOVERNMENT	**CLOSING OPPOSITION**
5. Member for the Government	6. Member for the Opposition
7. Government Whip	8. Opposition Whip

The debate is divided into eight speeches, with every speaker getting equal time (seven minutes). You will often hear speeches start with "Mr./Madam Chairperson" or "Mr./Madam Speaker" and end with "I beg to propose/oppose." Every speaker has a slightly different role. The Prime Minister must define the motion, explaining the course of action the Government wishes to take. The Leader of the Opposition should then set out the alternative position of his team. The two deputies must support their respective partners, while adding new arguments. The Members, while supporting the case made by the Opening team on their side, should find new, interesting, and important points to move the debate along. The Whips are primarily summary speakers who should present and characterize the story of the debate in favor of their side.

Debaters can interrupt speeches with Points of Information, brief comments, or questions put to a speaker on the opposing side, which she must respond to directly. They can challenge the argument a speaker is making, point out an apparent contradiction, highlight a point that the interrupter intends to make in her speech—anything that forwards the cause of the person asking and makes life uncomfortable for the respondent. Points of Information are made standing up—because the speaker usually rejects them, you will see people jumping up and down during each of the speeches.

A timekeeper enforces speech times as well as the time period in which Points of Information can be made. Points of Information cannot be offered during the opening and closing minutes of a speech. After one minute of each speech, the timekeeper should clap or bang on the table once—to notify speakers on the other side that they may offer Points of Information. The noise can be a shock to newcomers! The timekeeper should bang again after six minutes, ending the period during which Points of Information can be offered. After seven minutes, he should bang twice and the speaker should bring his speech to a close as soon as possible.

Although people speak as individuals, they are judged as teams of two, making the same case and supporting each other's arguments. The best team and the worst team in the debate may be on the same side.

When you watch debates, notice how much effort participants make to structure their speeches and label their points. You can learn a great deal from seeing experienced debaters at their best. But do not copy these speakers. When you hold your own debates, try to keep to the basic rules and conventions. But please speak in your own style, using vocabulary and arguments that make sense to you.

Debate requires diversity—not everyone speaking with one voice. I come across so many new debaters who set out by learning jargon words like *rebuttal* (for arguments that counter those previously made by the other side), *constructive* (meaning arguments), and *extension* (for a new argument) and using them a lot in their speeches. Often they speak very quickly, having seen a debate online that featured speeches delivered at high speed. My opinion is that those debates they have seen were good *despite* that jargon and high speed, not because of them. The best debaters, like the best communicators in any field, have a voice that is authentically theirs.

Developing a Successful Club

The key ingredients for success are involving everyone, setting good motions, and a commitment to coaching. For your club to flourish, you must not only hold debates but also encourage as many people as possible to participate in those debates. By sharing out the roles of Chair, timekeeper, speakers, floor speakers, and adjudicators, you can involve a great number of people in a single debate.

Ideas that have boosted numbers and interest in many clubs include: inviting a famous person to come and chair the debate; giving a prize for the best floor speech; giving a prize to the best new speaker. The University of Leeds once had the speaker of the House of Commons chair a debate, thus attracting enormous interest and attendance.

You can also encourage growth by being careful about team pairings. Often friends want to be on the same team. The most accomplished speakers may want to speak together. Debating is competitive and people like to win. Even so, it is better for the group if you pair experienced with inexperienced speakers, so the latter can learn from the former. Debating with different partners exposes you to a range of approaches and ideas that help you to learn.

Setting motions carefully is a crucial part of establishing a successful club. Choose topics that motivate a range of students to attend. Talking about international law every week will turn off a large number of your potential attendees. Pick a motion that is current, exciting, controversial, and that people want to talk about.

Wording a motion well is also important. If you want to debate human rights, setting the motion as "This House Would Protect Human Rights" is a mistake. With novice speakers, you are likely to get a debate where Government tells you genocide is bad and

Opposition agrees genocide is bad but says we shouldn't protect the right to free speech. What are they supposed to say—they will argue—genocide is good?

It is better to be specific—"This House Would Cut Aid to Countries That Abuse Human Rights" or "This House Would Abolish Blasphemy Laws." Then you are more likely to get the debate you want, not two sides arguing about what the debate is really about. A debate about a debate is the most tedious way you can spend an hour and should be avoided at all costs.

If you have a mixed-ability group in terms of mastery of language, make sure you don't confuse English-language skills with debating potential. Fluency in English is certainly a plus, but even with a limited vocabulary and less than perfect fluency, it is possible to make a point clearly, succinctly, and comprehensibly. When you are judging, do not penalize a debater for less-than-perfect command of English. Do penalize if it is impossible to understand what she is saying—but that goes for anyone, be they speakers of English as their mother tongue or as a second language.

Most debate clubs I have encountered have at least some members who speak English as a second language (ESL). At Worlds, as you would expect, dozens of speakers apply to be considered as ESL or EFL (English as a Foreign Language), which suggests an even lower level of exposure to English. People whose first language is not English compete alongside native speakers of English and often beat them. In 2004, a team from the University of Utrecht, in the Netherlands, won the European Championships. So don't underestimate the potential of nonnative speakers.

Coaching is another way in which your club can improve and grow. I look at approaches and techniques in greater detail in the chapter on training. As an overview, there are three main approaches: self-teaching, student-led coaching, and formal coaching. The first is the old-fashioned way, allowing each person to find his or her own path to improvement, learning from experience. Some of the most charismatic and brilliant speakers I have seen were self-taught. Competition is all some people need to succeed. But most clubs now try to offer a structured means to pass on knowledge and skills. Student-led coaching involves those who have managed to gain experience, perhaps from speaking or judging competitions, sharing their knowledge with the group. It is not an expert–novice divide, as all are still eager to improve, but a way of raising the overall group level by pooling know-how. A formal coach can be either a member of staff or an ex-debater brought in to run training sessions and manage the club. If you have access to someone with experience of WS debating, it can be a real advantage in accelerating your learning. I don't believe any one of these approaches is best. Every individual is different.

In short, the answer to "What do we need to get started?" is "Less than you think." You need a basic understanding of how a debate works, a willingness to try out different speaking and listening exercises, exciting motions that bring people in to participate in debates, and an open and welcoming environment.

2

How to Debate

In one sense, the answer is "You stand up, and you start talking." In another, more important sense, the answer is a very long way from that. A lot of mental groundwork should be laid before a single word is uttered. Your task is not just to make sense. It is to tell a story that gives an account of the whole debate, showing how the sides bind together and where your case fits into the whole.

It takes skill. Sometimes you speak first, sometimes eighth. From these different vantage points, you need to keep command of your case, the arguments you support, those you reject, back-up positions, how it all fits together. When you make or reject arguments, you must do so with rigor and clarity. You need to structure your speech and deliver it with style. You have to learn to handle situations, respond to the brilliance or failures of others, and keep listening to the debate while developing your own thoughts. You need to commit to your speech at the last possible moment to ensure that you are relevant. So, before you stand up and start talking, sit down, start thinking, and get listening.

This chapter will help you make best use of preparation time. It will teach you how to define a motion to create a clear debate. It will show how to build a case and to adapt to your unique role in the debate. We then get into the dirty work—how to make arguments well, to create clash between the two sides, to rebut and make Points of Information. Finally, we look at manner—how to use style, structure, language, and framing to get your message across.

Preparation Time

The hall goes quiet. The Chief Adjudicator announces that the final will start in 15 minutes. Everyone stares at the PowerPoint, waiting. Words jump out of the screen. You realize that you only have a quarter of an hour to make sense of the motion, think up a case, come up with great arguments, consider what others will say, and put it all together. And hundreds of people are watching. Gulp.

To those who have never debated or those used to styles where speakers get a week for research, the short period available to think through your speech is the most astonishing aspect of WS debating. How can people talk about an unfamiliar topic with so little preparation?

The answer is to use your time effectively. The only resources at your disposal are 1) your partner and 2) any written material you brought with you. The rules clearly prohibit conferring with anyone else, whether they are your coach, your Mom, your best friend, or an international law expert on the phone. You are not allowed to search for information on the Internet or use any electronic device at all.

This rule has only two exceptions. If you genuinely cannot understand a word or phrase in the motion, you should seek clarification from the person who announced it. At a tournament, this will be the Chief Adjudicator or one of her deputies. Second, if English is your second language, you are normally allowed to use an electronic dictionary to check the meaning of words that others use or that you want to use in your speech.

You and your partner need to work together to make the best use of your valuable time. Exactly how you use the time will depend on your position in the debate. If you are the Opening Government, you need to agree on a definition, a case, and the contents of the Prime Minister's speech, along with expected arguments for the second speaker. Any other position has many more possibilities. You need to think through all the possible definitions and cases that might be run by the Opening Government. For each of these scenarios, you need a response.

Imagine you are Opening Opposition for "This House Would Impose Sanctions on Barbaria." If the Opening Government defines sanctions as a UN-wide ban on all military, economic, and humanitarian interaction with Barbaria, that creates a totally different debate to a definition suggesting only sanctions on the bank accounts of the elite. Anticipating the first definition, you might have written down "sanctions will harm the poor," "sanctions will therefore cause a backlash against the West," "sanctions will leave them open to military invasion," and feel confident that you have arguments ready for deployment. Sadly, none of them are obvious responses to the second definition.

In my experience, unless you are in Opening Government, the best way to use the first 10 minutes of preparation time is to have a broad discussion of the ideas, issues, and examples you and your partner believe touch on the debate. The last five minutes can be used to make specific decisions about the case you would like to make in different scenarios and scoping out your arguments. But the final decision about your approach should be made only during the debate.

The alternative is to pore over written material. Some debaters like to build a casefile that contains notes from previous debates, ideas they had on all those topics, related articles, and background information. I have seen people use reference books to check statistics about a particular country's economy, ethnic divisions, religious groups, and other relevant features, particularly at international competitions.

Others bring a pile of newspapers or journals, hoping to get ideas or facts should something topical come up. Whereas you are unlikely to learn new concepts in 15 minutes, newspaper or magazine articles may contain background information or examples that add depth to your arguments. So long as this information is used in support of interesting, relevant arguments, it can be very helpful.

Let's say you are debating whether the European Union should expand to include Turkey. Knowing the Copenhagen Criteria for new members and the *acquis communautaire*, the accumulated legislation, legal acts, and court decisions that they are expected to adopt, could be helpful information. I say "could" because it depends on how the debate unfolds. While it might appear impressive to sound knowledgeable, your information does not defeat the argument that Turkey should be admitted regardless of current procedure or admitted as an explicit exception. Information supports arguments but it is no substitute for them. Debate is not a measure of how much you know. That is why I recommend spending your time thinking rather than trying to cram statistics into your head.

If you know nothing, then information is precious. But, in general terms, being over-prepared is worse than being underprepared. As an adjudicator, it is more common to see teams make preprepared arguments without regard to their impact on the debate, having apparently not listened to the Opening Government, than it is to see people just stop talking after five minutes because they can't think of anything more to say. You may fear having nothing to say and feel that saying anything at all is better than silence. To debate well, you need to take risks—postponing your commitment to your position to the last possible moment and ensuring that what you say is of maximum relevance to the live debate.

The final thought on preparation time is that you should prioritize the first speaker in the team. It is tempting to think up a few arguments and then split them neatly between the speakers, the precise division determined by the principle of equity or the relative knowledge base of your teammates. If your partner is an astrophysicist and the motion is about space exploration, why not give her all the complicated arguments about the practicalities of travel through the cosmos while you talk about cost and politics? Other popular ways that beginners create a division or "split," as it is sometimes called, are moral versus practical or political/economic/social. The problem with this is—again—that the debate may not turn out the way you expect it to. Your job is to make a case—to tell a story—that sounds convincing in light of the story told by the other side. If you tell the same story regardless of what the other side says, you are in danger of sounding confused or even irrelevant. That is why the first speaker must have the privilege and responsibility of choosing the best of your team's material when he or she stands up to speak. To an adjudicator, it is crucial that the first minute of your team's case makes sense. Any number of clever, innovative, and brilliant arguments are not going to win you a debate unless they are deployed as part of a winning case. So, the first speaker should make the best speech she can; the second speaker must listen carefully and then ensure that his own speech supports and adds to that of his teammate.

Throughout this section I have offered advice for how to use preparation time if you are *not* in Opening Government—being flexible, broad-minded, and ready for everything. If you are in Opening Government, you have total control over the first speech and can think through scenarios (How might they oppose this?) that enable you to plan the second speech as well. Preparation time is more focused because you are in charge of the beginning of the debate. Let's look at Opening Government's role in detail, starting with the initial task—defining the motion.

Definition

Defining the motion is a task unique to Opening Government. It is done by the Prime Minister, early in her speech, and, once accomplished, it replaces the original wording of the motion. Any attempts by other teams to return to the sentence read out by the Chief Adjudicator are invalid once a satisfactory definition has been made.

As the rules put it:

> The definition should state the issue (or issues) for debate arising out of the motion and state the meaning of any terms in the motion which require interpretation.

Usually, the definition gives an adequate starting point for the debate. Let's consider the motion "This House Would Ban the Physical Punishment of Children by Parents." The Prime Minister starts her speech by saying:

> *A parent who smacks their child's arm to keep her from immediate danger is acting out of necessity. A parent who smacks their child as a physical punishment, for something they did in the past, is acting out of cruelty. Children should be protected, through a new law, from this abuse by adults of their power.*

This opening makes clear what the PM means by "physical punishment." She distinguishes between a smack to avoid immediate danger and a smack given later in chastisement.

She is sketchy on the details of the new law; we don't know what happens to parents who are convicted. Also, no attempt has been made to delineate the ages of children covered, so we might presume coverage stretches from birth to 16 or perhaps 18. But the definition is fair and does the job.

Other teams are now bound by this definition. Closing Government cannot say, "We are only talking about parents who beat their children with belts or other implements," because Opening Government made clear that just a smack, when given in punishment, was sufficient to break their new law.

Opening Opposition cannot fairly say, "You will be putting parents in prison for keeping their children out of dangerous situations," because the Prime Minister made an exception in cases of immediate danger and did not establish whether prison is an option.

So far, so technical. You may have noticed that something is missing from the definition. It is entirely devoid of empathy. There is no sense that the Prime Minister feels anything when discussing the question of violence to children. In a persuasive environment, that is a peculiar way to behave.

A good definition is not simply a definition that follows the rules. It needs to make a powerful statement about why the debate matters, who is getting hurt, and what you are going to do about it.

> *The physical punishment of children by parents is abuse. It is a strong adult using his power to inflict harm on a defenseless child, a pattern of violence that is then passed on to future generations. If a mother smacks her child's arm to stop him touching boiling water, it is necessary. But if the father takes the child home and smacks him as a physical punishment, later, for going near the hot kettle, it is cruel. Children should be protected, through a new law, from this abuse by adults of their power.*

This is a better definition on a number of fronts. It has a strong initial statement, presaging arguments about the nature of abuse and the long-term harm caused by smacking. When those arguments appear, they will seem to fit, without the speaker having to say, "I am going to tell you...", signposting their points in a more obvious way.

The parent has moved from "they" to "he," which is more personal and suggestive. A man hitting a child is a stark image. The boiling water example gives a scenario we can all picture and understand intuitively.

Above all, it sounds like the Prime Minister cares about the topic. When you are coming up with a definition, check that it passes the "Who Cares?" test. This not only ensures that you are speaking with power, it will also help identify groups with a stake in this issue—in this instance, potentially: children, parents, foster parents, biological parents, the courts, the police, schools, the state, grandparents, babysitters, etc.

Definitions occasionally go wrong. When they do, the best idea is almost always to ignore that fact and try to get on with the debate. Appendix B—Definitional Challenges—gives a full account of the rules and practices that govern bad definitions.

Case

Every team, in every debate, should have a case. Their case is the story that they tell about the debate—what it is about, how the different viewpoints fit together, and why the judges should accept what they are saying about it. All the great debates I have seen contained four teams that each had a persuasive claim on these questions. Put simply, every team has their own story of why they have won the debate.

Technically, a case is a policy, course of action, or state of affairs that a team supports and the reasons for which they support it. When Opening Government lays out the first component at the start of the Prime Minister's speech, it is called their "definition." Opening teams must present a case that must include both policy and reasons. Closing teams support the same policy as their corresponding opening teams but for new reasons.

The overwhelming majority of debaters, in my experience, do not understand or accept the importance of having a case. Time after time in my role as an adjudicator, debaters have stared at me with mystified incomprehension as I explained that their case was weak. Often they have put to me that their arguments were excellent, that their rebuttal was incisive—as if those were the only two measures of debating excellence. One such heartbroken debater came to me after losing an Oxford semifinal and pleaded "but we had, like, eight solid arguments. They only had, like, five."

Giving feedback to such people is like asking someone why they didn't come to your costume party and being told—"Yeah, but I bought an outfit!—and I ordered a taxi! It was a really spectacular costume!—and the taxi was a Mercedes! I can't believe you didn't give me the best costume prize..." and so on. Arguments must hang together, create a compelling worldview, and take the listener on a journey that leads toward changing his or her mind.

Let me give you an example of how a speech without a case sounds.

Jane, speaking as member of the Government:

> *Mr. Speaker, we on Closing Government wish to begin by rebutting three points made by the Opening Opposition before going on to make two further points in support of our esteemed colleagues in Opening Government. The first thing they said was...*

This speech, so far, is all about process. It doesn't say what the Closing Government team thinks the debate is about, what the key issues are, how well the debate has gone so far, what the team plans to achieve. There is no attempt to characterize the debate, no sense of understanding the context within which the speech exists. We just know it will be a speech—a speech that follows the rules and conventions of debating to the letter. It is tedious.

A better example:

John, speaking as member of the Government:

> *Madam Speaker, listening to Opening Opposition, you would think that the government planned to attack Barbaria out of hatred or bloodlust; in Closing Government, we will show that the consequences of military intervention will be to prevent humanitarian disaster and create a better life for the people there. First, let me look at the three points outstanding from Opening Opposition...*

The two introductions are of roughly equal length. John's introduction achieves everything that Jane's achieves—but also says *what* the two new points are and *why* the team is making those points.

It is not just that they are new points and the rules say you have to make points that are new. It is specifically because the Opposition is claiming intervention will cause bloodshed that Closing Government wants to prove, in the long run, the opposite.

In her mind, the adjudicator now has John's team clocked as the "consequences team" or the "better life team." Knowing what the team is trying to persuade her of, the adjudicator has a way of assessing how successful the team is. If good arguments are made that support the prospect of averting humanitarian disaster and creating a better life, this team may have done well.

Why only "may" have done well? Because the case put to the adjudicators by Closing Government is based on Opening Opposition's claim that invading Barbaria will have negative consequences. Doing well on these consequences will likely place Closing Government ahead of Opening Opposition.

But let us assume that Closing Opposition makes moral arguments against the invasion of Barbaria, claiming that international law must be upheld whatever the consequences and backing up this case with detailed argument. What is then essential is that the Government Whip says something in response to the Closing Opposition case. He could claim that customary international law cannot help with this specific case, reject international law outright, show how the government's proposed actions fit within international law, or argue that the positive consequences make invasion worthwhile whatever international law says on paper. Whatever approach he takes, it is critical that he spend time explaining not only what he thinks about international law, but how important it is in this debate and why military action is still right in light of the new Opposition arguments.

If he does this, Closing Government will be doing very well. If he doesn't, then he has nothing more than a list of arguments. However sparkling and well delivered, they lose relevance if they say nothing about the new challenge posed by Closing Opposition.

So, the foundation of a case is a central statement—e.g., "Military intervention will prevent humanitarian disaster and create a better life for the people"—which is supported by your arguments. If you were forced to summarize the entirety of both Closing Government speeches in a single sentence (an excellent discipline!), this is the sentence you would come up with.

Upon that foundation, you need to show how your statement fits in with the other competing cases in the debate—so in addressing Closing Opposition in our Barbaria debate, the Government Whip may say, "An unclear and flawed body of international law, which spoke both ways in the cases of Kosovo and Iraq, should not take precedence over a clear analysis on the effects of military action and inaction."

Every speech you give should tell a story about the debate, creating a narrative and inviting the adjudicators to share it. Every time you speak, you should justify what you put in, and leave out, on grounds of relevance. As an adjudicator, whenever I hear debaters say they have three arguments and list them, the questions in my head are: "Why those three arguments?—To what end?—What is your case?"

Making a good case requires you to have thought comprehensively about the issues around a topic. Before you get into arguments, counterarguments, rebuttal, Points of Information, think:

- What is our case?
- How can we express it in a single sentence?
- How can we justify it?

Role

The other factor that will determine the shape of your case is your role or position in the debate. Each team has a subtly distinct set of required tasks to fulfill.

POSITION	SPEAKER 1	SPEAKER 2
Opening Government	defines the motion; lays out OG case; makes arguments	supports the OG case; makes arguments; rebuts
Opening Opposition	lays out OO case; makes arguments; rebuts	supports the OO case; makes arguments; rebuts
Closing Government	lays out CG case; makes arguments; rebuts	sums up debate; rebuts; new arguments (optional)
Closing Opposition	lays out CO case; makes arguments; rebuts	sums up debate; rebuts; no new arguments

Opening Government has the luxury of deciding exactly what course of action they want to propose, defining the motion, and laying out a case with arguments in support. This cannot be left to the second speaker. "I will tell you the benefits of legalizing prostitution and my partner will go on to tell you exactly how we will do it" is not a reasonable way to approach Opening Government. It leaves everyone guessing as to exactly what the debate is about. The first speaker should also avoid all temptation to rebut, in advance, presumed attacks from Opposition. You will either guess incorrectly and look wrong-footed or give them an idea—for which they will be grateful. The first speaker should use her time building the strongest possible case, dealing with all the practical issues, and leaving her partner to work on the rebuttal of Opening Opposition.

Opening Opposition's main job is to defeat Opening Government. Therefore, a large part of their role is characterizing and attacking the proposal from the other side. The position is not entirely negative, however. A common question at training events and briefings is: "Does Opening Opposition need a counter-prop?" —by which is meant a counter-proposal, a case that posits taking action. The answer is no—Opposition does not have to come up with an alternative plan. But Opening Opposition should say where they stand on the issue and try to defend that position with arguments. That position and the Government position should be mutually exclusive. It is no good coming up with an Opposition case that Government can agree with entirely.

If Opening Government is eager to invade Barbaria, the Opposition needs to say whether they would maintain sanctions on the country, leave it free to realize its nuclear ambitions, or some other idea. It is not enough, as debaters on Opposition sometimes assert, to say, "The burden on us is simply to show why your plan won't achieve what it says it will." You can only measure the success of a proposal by comparison with the alternatives. In life, sometimes we have only bad choices. Debaters are sometimes set variations on "This House Would Impose Peace in the Middle East"—the fact that no pair of student debaters has yet been able to devise a 14-minute plan to end all conflict between Israelis and Palestinians does not automatically give the victory to Opposition. So, while Opposition is in no way required to develop an alternative, deep, detailed plan, they should defend an alternative position. Usually, that position will be a variation on the status quo: We would give sanctions more time to work; we would step up the fight against prostitution rings; we would give more support to trafficked women.

Opening Opposition is advised to use a detailed counter-proposal only if necessary to create clash. When Opening Government is extremely unclear or chooses a very soft definition that leaves little room for disagreement, it can be helpful for Opposition to take a more assertive position. If "This House Would Impose Peace in the Middle East" were defined, softly and uncourageously, as "the U.S. should continue to pursue diplomatic channels to get both sides to the negotiating table," it would seem that the Proposition has missed the point about creating peace. In this instance, rather than just complaining—"You are supposed to be enforcing peace, not encouraging it, so we are going to agree with everything you said."—the Opening Opposition could take the harder line "we think the U.S. should cut off its aid and diplomatic ties, and leave them to it." The adjudicators will be grateful to you for creating a debate where it seemed there would be none.

Closing Government must have a case that is consistent with their colleagues on Opening Government. Morphing "we would bomb Barbaria" into "we would love bomb Barbaria" is a very quick route to fourth place. The trick for Closing Government, while being consistent, is to make a case that is new and important. It is not about doing something different, but doing the same thing for different reasons.

You can go deeper into consequences, assessing the effects on groups left out of the analysis so far, making causal links between actions now and future effects, bringing in evidence and case studies that lend weight to your views. You can give a deeper treatment to moral questions, getting beneath "freedom should trump equality" to consider why and the implications of those stances. There are always new things to say about a topic. Your job is to find them, highlight their novelty, and make them central to the debate. When the adjudicators sit down and discuss the debate, you want them to think the questions you raised were the key questions.

However poorly the Opening Government performs their role, Closing Government must refrain from openly criticizing their colleagues or changing their policy. Adjudicators are sympathetic to teams placed in a difficult position. Other teams will often use Points of Information to try to tie you explicitly to poor points made by the opening team. Just stand by the general case and refer them to your new and better arguments.

The second speaker on Closing Government is the only speaker who has a chance to respond to the Closing Opposition team. It is, therefore, crucial that she spend time addressing the case brought by Closing Opposition. This speech should be a summary of the whole debate, biased in favor of Government, and demonstrating the central importance of the Closing Government case. While it can contain new arguments, it is rarely a good idea to include them as they detract from your role—to make a complex debate simple.

Closing Opposition mirrors Closing Government. They must not contradict Opening Opposition. They must make a case that is new and important. The first speaker must not only talk about the proposal brought by Opening Government but the case of Closing Government as well—and find time to lay out their own case. The second speaker is strictly a summary speaker, drawing together the threads of the debate, demonstrating that the Opposition won and that Closing Opposition had the best case.

Once your case is settled and your role understood, it is time to consider arguments.

Arguments

If you have just flipped through the book until you reached this page, you are a typical debater! Arguments—logical points supporting a case—are the building blocks of a speech and debaters feel comfortable only when they have plenty of them.

For the final of the Edinburgh IV in 2001, I set the motion "This House Would Allow Parents to Decide How to Split Maternity and Paternity Leave." One of the finalists, a seasoned debater, surprised to encounter a topic he hadn't considered before, paced the corridors in an agitated state asking passersby, aloud, "What are the arguments?"

Around that time, there was a brief vogue for toting a book titled *Pros and Cons* that contained arguments on a wide range of topics.

The fashion for cramming arguments ended because it didn't work. You can't just identify "the arguments" on any topic and recite them. A speech is not just a collection of individual arguments, any more than a novel is just a collection of chapters.

Arguments work when they are deployed in furtherance of a case or, as the rules put it, "matter should be relevant, logical and consistent." Not just logical and consistent, but relevant. As we have seen, your case is the standard by which adjudicators assess your arguments. It is not the number of points you make nor even their quality, but the point they together prove that persuades others and will win you debates.

So, as you sit with your teammate and a blank sheet of paper during preparation time, before you start writing arguments, write down your case—a single sentence that sums up what you will bring to the debate.

That done, feel free to brainstorm arguments. Just pour out ideas without assessing them. Be creative. Once you have exhausted these original ideas, take a look at your list in light of your case. The questions you and your partner need to ask yourself are:

- Which arguments seem most important?

- Are any of them linked? If so, put them together. (e.g., three about the effects of invading Barbaria on the region)

- Are any of them inconsistent? (e.g., two about moral values, one saying that freedom is paramount, the other social cohesion)

If you do find inconsistencies, work them out of your case. Your story must make sense. If you can find weaknesses, your opponents certainly will!

Types of Argument

Once you have decided which arguments to deploy, cross-check against the different types of argument on this list.

ARGUMENT TYPE	QUESTION
Problem	What—specifically—is the problem and why does it matter?
Policy	What—specifically—should happen and who should do it?
Principles	Is it the right thing to do?—and on what basis?
Practicalities	Can it be implemented?—and how?
Consequences	How will it affect, directly and indirectly, positively and negatively, all the stakeholders?

Your case should say something about all five of these big questions. Think of their absence as trip wires preventing your case from being accepted by the adjudicators. Let me demonstrate this by working backward.

Debater (says):

> *The minority peoples of Barbaria will be freed from an oppressive regime and able to embrace real democracy, just as the people of Iraq and Afghanistan now elect their governments. In many ways a successful democratic transition is more likely. There is a recent tradition of democracy, a strong trade union movement, underground opposition parties, and a civil society that has remained surprisingly robust despite recent oppression, as seen in the recent Million March for freedom.*

Adjudicator (thinks):

> Yes, that's all very plausible but Barbaria has developed nuclear weapons—we can't possibly invade.

The speaker has made a persuasive argument about the *consequences* of a successful invasion. But the team hasn't yet done the groundwork of proving an invasion would be successful. Let's revisit the speech.

Debater (says):

> *It is widely accepted that Barbaria has acquired a nuclear capability. But because the country lacks the missile technology to launch a warhead, Barbaria is not yet in a position to use its weapons against an invader. Independent analysts like IARA claim that the development of nuclear weapons is due to fears about the relative weakness of their armed forces. And the very weakness of its armed forces that led to nuclear development will make it easier for our mission to succeed.*
>
> *The minority peoples of Barbaria will be freed from an oppressive regime and able to embrace real democracy, just as the people of Iraq and Afghanistan now elect their governments.*

*In many ways a successful democratic transition is more likely.
There is a recent tradition of democracy, a strong trade union
movement, underground opposition parties, and a civil society
that has remained surprisingly robust despite recent oppression,
as seen in the recent Million March for freedom.*

Adjudicator (thinks):

I can see how this would work though I wonder what the
Opposition will say about Barbaria's supposed inability to
deploy warheads. It seems plausible that they could transition to democracy more easily than Iraq or Afghanistan. But
it is just wrong to go around toppling basically democratic
regimes like Barbaria. They are ignoring this enormous
difference!

The speaker has now grounded the likely *consequences* for Barbaria on an account of the *practicalities* of invasion. But the adjudicator still feels a big part of the jigsaw is missing. We need to build in
something about *principles*.

Debater (says):

*Some say Barbaria is a democracy. If it is, it is a democracy where
a powerful majority brutally suppresses weak minorities. Elections are fraudulent and violent. The media are state-controlled
and slavishly partisan. Popular demonstrations of opposition
are met with army violence. We, in Government, argue that Barbaria is not a real democracy. But even if it were, the threat made
by its president to attack and wipe out its neighbors, allied with
its recent acquisition of nuclear weapons, means that we must
take immediate action to overthrow his regime.*

*It is widely accepted that Barbaria has acquired a nuclear
capability. But because the country lacks the missile technology
to launch a warhead, Barbaria is not yet in a position to use its
weapons against an invader. Independent analysts like IARA
claim that the development of nuclear weapons is due to fears
about the relative weakness of their armed forces. And the very*

weakness of its armed forces that led to nuclear development will make it easier for our mission to succeed.

The minority peoples of Barbaria will be freed from an oppressive regime and able to embrace real democracy, just as the people of Iraq and Afghanistan now elect their governments. In many ways a successful democratic transition is more likely. There is a recent tradition of democracy, a strong trade union movement, underground opposition parties, and a civil society that has remained surprisingly robust despite recent oppression, as seen in the recent Million March for freedom.

Having linked together *principles, practicalities,* and *consequences,* the speaker has a stronger, broader appeal. (Prefaced with an introduction that covers *problem* and *policy,* e.g.:)

Any country that threatens its neighbors with nuclear weapons should be stopped. If it can be stopped peacefully, with sanctions, then that should be the course. In the case of Barbaria, sanctions have been tried and sanctions have failed. We are left with only one available course: Military intervention by a coalition including the U.S., UK, and others to overthrow the president of Barbaria and implement real democracy.

Some say Barbaria is a democracy...

If you read through the whole, you get a sense of arguments flowing into one another, supporting each other. The passage has jumped over the potential trip wires. It still needs more and deeper arguments, the links between them must be strengthened, and more evidence would be useful. Think of all the potential consequences —to Barbaria, its neighbors, its minorities, its majority, its creditors, to the countries invading, to international law, to the UN, to other conflicts—just to name a few obvious ones! There is a lot of scope for further arguments.

All of these types of argument are relevant to any debate. Understanding and appreciating the different types of argument are critical skills. One flashpoint that can come about between debaters and adjudicators happens when a speaker spends his whole time persuading adjudicators that Opening Government's plan isn't practical—it will fail. "I proved conclusively it won't work—what more is there to say?" The answer is that it is even more persuasive to show that even if it *did* work, the *consequences* would be lamentable and the morality (principles) of the enterprise repugnant. You don't win golf tournaments with a single club, however good your swing, and you don't win debates with a single argument, however destructive its force.

Let's look in depth at the three most important types of argument. Once we get beyond definitional disputes over the problem and policy, the most fruitful areas for debate are principles, practicalities, and consequences.

PRINCIPLES

The default moral position for many debaters is a utilitarian position. Utilitarians believe that the value of actions derives solely from their consequences. If a course of action leads to more benefits than costs, the suggestion is that we are compelled to follow it. "Killing one terrorist with a bomb will save one hundred innocent people, so let's go ahead and do it." If we accept this reasoning, our arguments about principles and consequences all merge into the same set.

Taking other moral positions creates difficulties. If we feel moved to appeal that "life is sacred, so killing that one person is just wrong," we might fairly be asked on what basis we make that claim. Deriving moral authority from God's commandments makes it difficult to engage with those who deny that authority.

Human rights might be invoked as the basis for restraint in this case. But debaters opposite may be all too happy to reject the existence of human rights and challenge you to prove they exist. If you are relying on natural law, where does that come from?

We might appeal to Kantian principles, arguing that this extreme example of one versus one hundred should not divert us, that we must treat people as ends, not means, and behave in the way we would will the universal moral law—not killing the terrorist.

I would encourage you to learn and understand a range of moral positions, thinking through their foundations. It will help you to become more persuasive when articulating the reactions that many average reasonable people feel when encountering a case that entails death and suffering.

I would also encourage you to engage critically with the utilitarian norm in debating. To "Killing one person will save one hundred, so let's go ahead and do it," you might ask, "Where do you get the idea that all lives are of equal worth?" You could point out "as utilitarians, you surely believe that if those hundred innocent deaths caused a backlash that rooted out terrorism for good, then it would be better to save the terrorist and let the innocent hundred die."

In the end, barring divine intervention, no definitive resolution of differences in principle can be reached. But you can take three actions to make your principled case stronger:

1. Demonstrate that you are comfortable in your moral code, whatever that may be, and can work it down to its foundations. If your natural law defense of human rights is attacked, showing that you understand the difference between "killing" and "murdering," and its relevance here, will strengthen your argument.

2. Challenge the alternative moral code, demonstrating its perverse effects in its own terms as well as the reasons it fails in your terms. Utilitarianism is ripe with possibility here. It is great at telling you the score but very bad at telling you what it is measuring. Note that concepts like "innocence" and "guilt" have no place in utilitarian thinking, which derives all value from consequences. Your opponents, lazily labeling their point as "utilitarian" as a nod to intellect, may be surprised to be put on the defensive: "The same utilitarian reasoning says you should kill yourself and give your organs to save the lives of others—why are you still here? What makes a terrorist different?"

3. Root your case in specific examples that are of central importance to the debate. While there are cases of police shooting suspected terrorists in error, the scenario of the terrorist with the ticking bomb has not yet arisen in real life. If the whole debate is about the latter example, it will shape the ethical discussion by excluding the real-world side effects of a shoot-to-kill policy. Remember that your principles are there to enlighten the debate. The debate is not a thought experiment in which to explore the principles.

PRACTICALITIES

It is tempting to jump from policy to consequences, just as advertising tells us that buying sneakers will change our lives. The ethical questions about how the shoes are made are airbrushed away in an ad. The practical considerations—that I can't run half a mile without stopping, that I don't want to spend $100 on footwear—are similarly swept aside. In a debate, these nagging questions remain. We've looked at principles. Now let's consider practicalities.

Worlds Style debates are about policy. The question at stake is whether a government or some other body should take a particular course of action. Any action runs the risk of failure. Therefore, an appreciation of what is involved in the implementation of a policy is important to any debater.

Practicalities are always relevant but rarely decisive in a WS debate. Every idea has its weaknesses, every plan its faults. An unanswerable proposition would be undesirable in a debate. In fact, if Opening Government suggests taking action that has no reasonable opposition, that definition can be challenged by their opponents and penalized by the adjudicators.

The mark of inexperienced debaters is that they focus heavily on practicalities. In opening opposition to "This House Would Take a Risk for Peace in the Middle East," their eyes light up whenever references are made to negotiations or peaceful coexistence between Israel and Palestine. "First, the two sides won't agree. Second, extremists won't be bound in. Third, it will take ages and lose momentum."

These are genuine concerns. But debaters should be judicious about how far they push this line. The troubles in Northern Ireland were intractable until all parties came to an agreement that brought peace and political change. History is full of conflicts that have ended, enemies who have learned to live in peace.

So, alongside an insistence that something won't work, you need to consider a couple of possibilities.

First, what if you are wrong? This is a question I always put to teams who hang a great deal on their practical arguments. These "even if..." arguments are really important to make during the debate. "Even if you were able to persuade the leadership of Hamas to publicly recognize the state of Israel, it would lead to fractures within the movement and end up causing greater violence." As with any argument, you need to back up your point with reasoning and evidence. You do not have to choose between criticizing practicalities and arguing about the consequences predicted by your opponents. But use "even if..." to pivot from your worldview to theirs and back again.

Second, even if you are right, what does it matter? Even if both sides agree that no peaceful resolution is possible, there is room for a wide-ranging debate about how the various sides should behave in light of that fact. History does not stop because peace is not currently attainable. Peace is not the only possible measure of success —unless the debaters have all stumbled into being utilitarians. Is it morally better, in the absence of peace, that settlement building continue, that Hamas remain in control of Gaza—not "Is it conducive to peace?" but "Is it right?" Does the principle of restraint have any value?—not instrumentally, but as a guiding principle of human conduct?

Shining a rhetorical light on deep-seated practical problems might weaken the strength of arguments about consequences, but it does not necessarily have any impact on principled arguments.

CONSEQUENCES

In Worlds Style debates, the Government advocates change. This opens up a plethora of possible consequences. Like a pebble falling into a pond, any case you drop into the room will have ripple effects.

When you talk about consequences, think about the positives and the negatives. Make tactical concessions—rather than assuming that everything on your side is rosy and that the other side is paving the way to hell like some one-eyed politician. Picking out only the consequences that support your side is a dangerous game. "Legalizing prostitution will improve the safety of sex workers" is an argument I have heard many times. Fine, as far as it goes. But it needs more development. How many current sex workers will join the regulated market for sex? If only some, then we must qualify this to "some sex workers." What about the rest? What will the effects be on those who stay outside the regulated market and continue to work illegally (because they are on drugs or want to charge more for unsafe sexual practices). And, given a choice, will violent men choose to seek out regulated sex workers and run the higher risk of getting caught? No.

Because the argument is not adequately developed, the basic point—that prostitution should be legalized—is in danger of being horribly weakened by observations from the other side that demonstrate that it is too simplistic. In the adjudicator's mind, we have reached: "Legalizing prostitution will improve the safety of some sex workers, while others, who are on drugs or willing to engage in unsafe sexual practices, continue to work illegally and will continue to be attacked." This is not such a great argument.

So, make a tactical concession:

Not all sex workers will choose or be able to work in the regulated market. Some women will continue to be exploited. But we will be able to focus scarce police resources to work on this smaller problem. The vast majority will be safer. And, because they will be safer, there will be a continuing incentive to enter the regulated market.

This shows that you have understood that your plan has some problems but that you also have the ability to put them into context. Some people will continue to suffer, but there is a carrot and stick to help change that situation so they can join the many who will benefit.

This example highlights another common weakness in handling consequences: the crude division of people into groups. In the prostitution debate, the general statement "women will benefit" turns out to be "some women will benefit," at which point the queries "who," "how many," "in what ways," and "why" all become relevant and a new level of depth is unveiled.

Let's consider another debate: "This House Would Ban the Wearing of Religious Symbols in State Schools." Government often argues that "children will no longer be isolated or segregated by their religion." In fact, it is more complicated than that. Those children who remain in state schools after the ban might arguably be less segregated, but those who attend a single-faith private school or are taught at home as a result of the decision will be more segregated.

The trick is to identify all of the many possible types of response that different people will have to the passing of a certain law. There are always both intended and unintended consequences. Try to identify all of the different stakeholders and think through all of the ways in which they might react to the policy being considered.

Not only should your treatment of consequences be subtle and deeply considered, it should link to your arguments on principles and practicalities.

You could spend most of a speech persuading me that "children will no longer be isolated or segregated by their religion" as a consequence of your plan. But if you earlier told me "parents' right to choose the kind of education their children experience is paramount," then I will be confused about why you think it is bad for children to be segregated by their religion. And, if you said, in your definition, "teachers will give children a warning, but we will not physically remove the item," then I will question whether that is sufficient enforcement to stop children from flouting the law.

Consequences, practicalities, and principles all must be united in the furtherance of a case.

Making Arguments Well

Let's recap. You have a case, you have a bunch of arguments, you have picked the best ones, you have cross-checked them to ensure that you are making different types of argument. How do you make an argument well?

The first step is to *state* your point clearly. Consider this fragment from a debate about legalizing prostitution:

> *Lots of girls get into trouble—and boys sometimes, too—with problems at home or addiction—and they need money to survive so it isn't really—I mean, they do choose to do it in the sense that they aren't coerced into doing it, but starting from where they are, with all that has happened to them, it is hardly the same as stealing or robbing a bank or even committing welfare fraud.*

What is the point here? It isn't "lots of girls get into trouble," or "they need money to survive," or "they choose to do it," or "it is hardly the same as stealing." It is an unspoken point: "Prostitutes should not be treated as criminals." Because it is unspoken, you spend the whole time trying to piece it together rather than understanding it immediately and then considering it.

The second step is to *explain* the point clearly. "It is hardly the same as stealing or robbing a bank..."—why? The speaker accepts that people choose to be prostitutes. What is the distinction between choosing to break one law and choosing to break another? If the point is "prostitutes should not be treated as criminals," then what is the relevance of "lots of girls get into trouble... and they need money to survive"? After all, people who steal and those who engage in welfare fraud are treated like criminals despite the fact that they may have problems at home, addictions, and need money to survive. We may feel sympathetic to their plight, but the point has not been proved.

Let's try to make the point again.

> *Prostitutes should not be treated as criminals. Lots of girls get into trouble—and boys sometimes, too—with problems at home or addiction—and they need money to survive. Choosing to rob a bank, steal or committing welfare fraud is rightly criminalized. Choosing instead to work for a living—in one of the most unpleasant and dangerous jobs you can do—should not be treated the same way. It is right to choose hard work over stealing and the law should support people who make that choice.*

We can quickly understand the point that is being made and the reasoning that backs up the point. There is scope for much greater depth—after all, prostitution may be better than stealing but still is wrong, just as stealing is better than murder but still is wrong; there may be other reasons to criminalize prostitution. But as a statement of the original point, it is greatly improved.

In competitive debating, *stating* and *explaining* are the key to getting your points across effectively. Without a good command of logic and evidence, your points will not convince adjudicators. But you should not overlook *illustrating* your points as well.

Imagine if debaters did TV advertising. Pet charities would seek donations by showing experts explaining a graph containing a trend analysis of the numbers of animal cruelty incidents. Why show a dog? You know what one looks like! Cute puppets and cartoon characters would never front insurance commercials as they lack credibility. Luxury cars wouldn't be shown racing around open mountain roads—there are very few mountain roads and anyway it's only one car, it doesn't prove anything.

In the real world, however, illustrations are what persuade people, moving them to act. They enrich an argument, grounding it in our everyday experiences, giving it a human element that brings it alive. Debating in generalities, referring to "those people," "the girls," "collateral damage," "negative externalities" or any of the other academic ways we dehumanize our language—all have an effect on your ability to communicate. While it is usually inappropriate to use an anecdote—how can somebody argue against your personal experience?—it is important to ground your arguments in real life.

Returning to our prostitution argument, here's how it could look with greater illustration:

> Prostitutes should not be treated as criminals. Sixteen-year-old girls and boys, abused at home, possibly addicted to drugs, need money to survive. If they chose to rob a bank, steal, or commit welfare fraud, they would rightly be prosecuted. If they choose instead to work for a living—in one of the most unpleasant and dangerous jobs they could do—they should not be punished for it. It is right to choose hard work over stealing, and the law should support the desperate young people who make that choice.

Being more specific about the people whose lives you are discussing animates this point. Compare it with the earlier versions. They are more general, vague, and discuss prostitution as if it were a handy forum for applying theoretical principles rather than a moving human issue. Illustrating the point has not weakened the argument—or lengthened it. It has strengthened it by making it more persuasive.

In summary, arguments should each be clearly stated, explained, and illustrated. Together, they should support a case that is clear and distinct from the cases of other teams in the debate. That case should cover all angles of the issue: the problem being discussed, the solution suggested, the principles at stake, the practicalities entailed, and the consequences produced. The ability to wield arguments in pursuit of a comprehensive case lies at the heart of successful debating.

Clash

Debates cannot be won by a brilliant case alone. A debate is a contest where you need to characterize other teams and deal with other arguments, showing where your ideas clash with the rest.

Clash refers to the points of disagreement in a debate, where the two sides come into conflict. Given that the objective of a debate is for those listening to accept or reject a motion, there is no avoiding disagreement in a debate. In fact, where debaters try to shy away from saying anything controversial or define away areas of disagreements, they are punished. Good debaters welcome clash as the opportunity to test and prove their case against all opposing views.

At the macro level, clash is about commenting on how your case fits in with other cases. Remember this example:

> Member for the Government: *Madam Speaker, listening to Opening Opposition, you would think that the Government planned to attack Barbaria out of hatred or bloodlust; in Closing Government, we will show that the consequences of military intervention will be to prevent humanitarian disaster and create a better life for the people there. First, let me look at the three points outstanding from Opposition...*

Note how it dovetails the case of Closing Government with the case put by Opening Opposition. If this characterization of

Opposition's case is a fair one in the minds of the adjudicators, then Closing Government has managed to demonstrate clash in the first 15 seconds of their first speech. By next going through systematically and proving each point, they can do real damage to Opening Opposition.

And remember the alternative:

> *Mr. Speaker, we on Closing Government wish to begin by rebutting three points made by Opening Opposition before going on to make two further points in support of our esteemed colleagues in Opening Government. The first thing they said was . . .*

This just says to the adjudicators that "we're going to disagree with stuff they said. We won't tell you why. We won't tell you how it fits into the big picture. Insofar as we have a case, you're going to have to figure it out for yourself as we go along."

Having established a case and how it fits with other accounts of the debate, you might think I will—finally—let you get on with the fun stuff and start rebutting arguments. Not so fast.

In a Worlds Style debate, there is no expectation that every point made by the opposing side should be rebutted. The idea is that you prioritize, distinguishing between the more important points, to which you will devote a great deal of time, and the less important, which you will dismiss either in passing or not address at all. There is also a third category, consisting of those points made by the other side that you agree with.

The counterpart error to rushing to "the arguments" is rushing to "the rebuttal," as if they were boxes to be checked off on an adjudicator's score sheet. You need to synthesize ideas and prioritize before you speak.

Because the purpose of rebuttal is to demonstrate clash between cases, you need to use your judgment to decide which of these three categories each of the arguments fits into.

Let's look again at the very simple case we built up for invading Barbaria and think about how we, as Opposition, could respond to it:

> Government: *Any country that threatens its neighbors with nuclear weapons should be stopped. If it can be stopped peacefully, with sanctions, then that should be the course. In the case of Barbaria, sanctions have been tried and sanctions have failed. We are left with only one available course: Military intervention by a coalition including the U.S., UK, and others, to overthrow the president of Barbaria and implement real democracy.*
>
> *Some say Barbaria is a democracy. If it is, it is a democracy where a powerful majority brutally suppresses weak minorities. Elections are fraudulent and violent. The media are state-controlled and slavishly partisan. Popular demonstrations of opposition are met with army violence. We, in Government, argue that Barbaria is not a real democracy. But even if it were, the threat made by its president to attack and wipe out its neighbors, allied with its recent acquisition of nuclear weapons, means that we must take immediate action to overthrow his regime.*
>
> *It is widely accepted that Barbaria has acquired a nuclear capability. But because the country lacks the missile technology to launch a warhead, Barbaria is not yet in a position to use its weapons against an invader. Independent analysts like IARA claim that the development of nuclear weapons is due to fears about the relative weakness of their armed forces. And the very weakness of its armed forces that led to nuclear development will make it easier for our mission to succeed.*
>
> *The minority peoples of Barbaria will be freed from an oppressive regime and able to embrace real democracy, just as the people of Iraq and Afghanistan now elect their governments. In many ways a successful democratic transition is more likely. There is a recent tradition of democracy, a strong trade union movement, underground opposition parties, and a civil society*

that has remained surprisingly robust despite recent oppression, as seen in the recent Million March for freedom.

Looking at the very first sentence, *"Any country that threatens its neighbors with nuclear weapons should be stopped,"* we have choices on opposition.

POSITION 1—"We agree that any country that threatens its neighbors with nuclear weapons should be stopped—but Barbaria is not a threat to its neighbors."

POSITION 2—"We agree that any country that threatens its neighbors with nuclear weapons should be stopped—but Barbaria does not have nuclear weapons."

POSITION 3—"Dictatorships that threaten their neighbors should be stopped, but democracies should not and Barbaria is a democracy."

POSITION 4—"It is not for us in the West to decide who gets to have nuclear weapons and how they should pursue their foreign policy."

POSITION 5—"We agree that any country that threatens its neighbors with nuclear weapons should be stopped and that Barbaria is threatening its neighbors with nuclear weapons."

Positions 1 and 2 question the very basis of the debate—if you remember, similar objections were raised (substituting weapons of mass destruction [WMD] for nuclear weapons) against the invasion of Iraq in 2003.

Positions 3 and 4 create clash by turning the debate into a disagreement about the circumstances under which it is right to intervene.

Position 5 doesn't create clash—yet. But if we go through the rest of Government's first paragraph—

Any country that threatens its neighbors with nuclear weapons should be stopped. If it can be stopped peacefully, with sanctions, then that should be the course. In the case of Barbaria, sanctions have been tried and sanctions have failed. We are left with only one available course: Military intervention by a coalition including the U.S., UK, and others, to overthrow the president of Barbaria and implement real democracy.

—there is plenty of scope for disagreement

POSITION 5A—"We agree that any country that threatens its neighbors with nuclear weapons should be stopped and that Barbaria is threatening its neighbors with nuclear weapons, BUT we believe sanctions on Barbaria are working/will work."

POSITION 5B—"We agree that any country that threatens its neighbors with nuclear weapons should be stopped and that Barbaria is threatening its neighbors with nuclear weapons AND that sanctions have failed, BUT we believe a U.S./UK-led mission would be doomed to failure and only a UN-mandated force should be sent."

Considering the potential that exists to combine these positions, you have extraordinary scope for creating a whole range of very different debates out of just the few lines uttered by the first speaker.

The decision to adopt a position will inform what and how you rebut. Let's look at how you would shape your rebuttal if you took Position 5b. Look again at the paragraph, claiming Barbaria is not a real democracy.

Some say Barbaria is a democracy. If it is, it is a democracy where a powerful majority brutally suppresses weak minorities. Elections are fraudulent and violent. The media are state-controlled and slavishly partisan. Popular demonstrations of opposition are met with army violence. We, in Government, argue that Barbaria is not a real democracy. But even if it were, the threat made by its president to attack and wipe out its neighbors, allied with its recent acquisition of nuclear weapons, means that we must take immediate action to overthrow his regime.

Does it matter to you on opposition? Had you taken position 3, you would need to focus a lot of attention on the question of democracy. But the answer for you is no—you are committed to take action against any country that is doing what both sides say Barbaria is doing. So don't spend a long time articulating your position. Just say you agree and invite the Government to focus on where you disagree what kind of force is best.

Maintaining position 5b, look at the argument that invasion is credible.

> It is widely accepted that Barbaria has acquired a nuclear capability. But because the country lacks the missile technology to launch a warhead, Barbaria is not yet in a position to use its weapons against an invader. Independent analysts like IARA claim that the development of nuclear weapons is due to fears about the relative weakness of their armed forces. And the very weakness of its armed forces that led to nuclear development will make it easier for our mission to succeed.

You may happen to know that IARA is a made-up organization, a figment of the imagination of Proposition. But their argument—that military invasion is easy—helps your case that the U.S. and UK are not needed. You have no reason to mention their error. Undermining their argument, in this instance, would weaken yours.

Continuing with position 5b, look at the final paragraph, claiming that the consequences of invasion will be a swift democratic transition.

> The minority peoples of Barbaria will be freed from an oppressive regime and able to embrace real democracy, just as the people of Iraq and Afghanistan now elect their governments. In many ways a successful democratic transition is more likely. There is a recent tradition of democracy, a strong trade union movement, underground opposition parties, and a civil society that has remained surprisingly robust despite recent oppression, as seen in the recent Million March for freedom.

You might well choose to spend time rebutting these points, arguing that a Western-led invasion will lead to violence and rejection of a new regime imposed without a UN mandate.

One Government case presents multiple possibilities for Opposition. The job of the Opposition speakers is to analyze and make strategic choices about how to oppose—not simply to disagree with everything their opponents say.

The guiding principle is to create clash between the two sides —to decide where disagreements should fall and to argue such key points really well.

Clash involves a lot more than simply rebutting points, just as building a case involves more than just making arguments. Not only do you need to identify where the two sides differ, you need to pick out the most important differences. As well as arguing that they are wrong, you need to explain what your position would be even if they were right. You need to be ready to ask and respond to Points of Information at any stage of the debate. Clash is ever-present and what makes debate—at its best—an exciting live event.

Rebuttal

Finally, it is time to rebut. I hope it proves worth the wait! In rebutting, you need to identify clearly your opponent's point, take it at its strongest, and argue your objection. Looking at the third paragraph of Government's argument about invading Barbaria, compare the following three rebuttal statements:

> Government: *It is widely accepted that Barbaria has acquired a nuclear capability. But because the country lacks the missile technology to launch a warhead, Barbaria is not yet in a position to use its weapons against an invader. Independent analysts like IARA claim that the development of nuclear weapons is due to fears about the relative weakness of its armed forces. And the very*

weakness of its armed forces that led to nuclear development will make it easier for our mission to succeed.

REBUTTAL 1: "They said something about being easy to invade and having missiles, but we saw from Iraq and Afghanistan it's not as straightforward as all that."

REBUTTAL 2: "So the fact it has nuclear weapons means it's going to be easier to invade? Brilliant. Next stop Pyongyang, guys."

REBUTTAL 3: "The Prime Minister said Barbaria lacks missile technology. That's an enormous gamble with the lives of our troops given 1) how secretive the regime is, 2) the fact that this is an enormous military secret they are unlikely to reveal to us, and 3) our woeful track record predicting other countries' WMD capabilities."

Rebuttal 1 is unclear and confused. Exactly what point is being opposed? On what grounds? This is just a bit of general sniping, raising doubts without analyzing the argument.

Rebuttal 2 is designed to raise a laugh and would probably play well with an audience. The difficulty is that it doesn't address the argument made—that we should conclude from the development of nuclear weapons that Barbaria's conventional weapons are weak —but just plays on its counter-intuitive reasoning.

Rebuttal 3 is better. It targets a specific claim—that Barbaria lacks missile technology. It then raises specific questions about the claim, suggesting that we don't know it to be true and the risks of getting it wrong could lead to catastrophe.

You should take the same care for accuracy with your rebuttal as you do with your arguments. Adjudicators are listening carefully to both sides, so if you dismiss lightly arguments made by the other side, they will notice. Of course, mockery is permitted and can be effective if the point targeted really was poor. The key is to avoid distorting points to make them easier to attack. Instead, assume the very best of a point before you knock it down.

In summary, the arguments you rebut should depend on the case you put forward. Rebuttal is not just a list of points about which you disagree. If you agree, say so. If your differences are irrelevant, minimize the time you spend on them. Focus on the big distinctions between the two sides. Attack points at their strongest, not at their weakest.

Even if . . .

A debater needs to be flexible enough to operate in more than one world. Her own worldview—the one expressed in her case—will take her some of the way. The rest is achieved by entering the worldview of other teams and showing their inadequacies.

This skill normally takes form in a sentence starting "even if." "Even if" allows you to engage with more of your opponent's case without having to make concessions.

Consider this passage of rebuttal again:

> *The Prime Minister said Barbaria lacks missile technology. That's an enormous gamble with the lives of our troops given 1) how secretive the regime is, 2) the fact that this is an enormous military secret they are unlikely to reveal to us, and 3) our woeful track record predicting other countries' WMD capabilities.*

And then add this to it:

> *But even if he is right about missiles, nuclear material, which we know they possess, could easily be added to dirty bombs and other devices used against our troops. And even if they decide against using the material, they may sell it to terrorist groups to raise money and ensure that it doesn't fall into our hands.*

The speaker doesn't say, "There *are* missiles" and leave it at that. She says, "Even if there weren't missiles, you would still be in the wrong." This is a stronger position.

We use "even if..." when we want to demonstrate problems with a view that we do not hold. In the example above, the speaker doesn't just say, "You're wrong about missiles" or "It's irrelevant what you say about missiles because..." By stating, "Even if he is right about missiles," she doesn't have to concede her point before engaging with the hypothetical situation. Her stance is: "You're wrong; even if you were right, you would be wrong."

We can sometimes take an even stronger position. If the other side is putting a case or argument that fits within our worldview, we can agree with them and co-opt their point. Let's say I propose legalizing drugs, whereas you oppose with the case that we should educate children more about the dangers of drugs. It is entirely reasonable that I say we should do both. They are not mutually exclusive.

The power of using "even if..." in debates is that it opens up a world of clash by allowing you to delve more deeply into your opponent's world. Rather than saying, "It won't work...so that's all there is to say about it," you can take a more holistic view—"It won't work, but even if it did work, it would cause greater suffering."

Points of Information (POIs)

Points of Information (questions directed to the person speaking) are an opportunity to subject your opponents to instant examination. Answering a POI is a chance to demonstrate your total command of subject matter under fire. Here are the rules on handling Points of Information:

- Points of Information may be asked between the first-minute mark and the six-minute mark of a speech (where speeches are of seven minutes duration). Points of Information should only be directed to speakers on the other side of the table.

- To ask a Point of Information, a debater should stand, placing one hand on his or her head and extend the other toward the member speaking. In practice, many people just stand up and stick out their hand without touching the head.

- The debater may announce that he would like to ask a "Point of Information" or use other words to this effect, such as "on that point." Slipping in bits of your intended point by saying, e.g., "On Burma," is not allowed.

- The debater who is speaking may accept or decline to answer the Point of Information.

- Points of Information should not exceed 15 seconds in length.

- The member who is speaking may ask the person offering the Point of Information to sit down once he has had a reasonable opportunity to be heard and understood.

- Members should attempt to answer at least two Points of Information during their speech. Members should also offer Points of Information.

So, why should you bother offering and answering POIs? A debate is a live event, not a public speaking competition; the traditions of Worlds Style debate are the cut and thrust of British Parliamentary debating, with interruptions and hostile questioning possible at any stage.

Points of Information are used for a variety of reasons. A point can be used to clarify the meaning of an argument or the significance of something said within an argument—"So, you think it's acceptable to allow under-18s to go into prostitution?" It can be used to draw attention to a contradiction or tension between two points made by the same speaker, team, or side—"Earlier you said Barbaria was oppressive, now you say it's bursting with liberty and a free civil society—which is it?" It can be deployed to introduce an idea that you want to speak about later or to remind everyone of arguments you made earlier—"What do you think the effects of legalization would be on the children of prostitutes?" or "What, then, do you say to our point that a prolonged guerrilla war is the most likely outcome?"

POIs can be effective in different ways. They can highlight weaknesses in an opponent's case by demonstrating that your opponent hasn't thought through the full implications of their position. They can force a speaker to deal with an issue she hadn't considered. They can highlight the centrality of your points to the debate, reminding adjudicators of your continued participation.

The best points are succinct and clear. They are usually questions —but don't have to be formulated as a question as long as they challenge the person speaking. Ideally, they are related to the argument being made by the person speaking, adding spontaneity to the debate.

Adjudicators will note Points of Information and should reward you for asking challenging, interesting points as part of their overall assessment of the debate.

You have more to lose than to gain from answering Points of Information. The best case has you responding to an unexpected point by offering a sparkling, witty reply, then returning seamlessly to your argument. If you do, it will raise the level of an excellent speech. The worst case finds you standing, mouth open, wondering what was meant, muttering something about answering it later, leaving it to your partner, or pretending you haven't heard it.

You can avoid trouble with Points of Information by remembering only to accept them at a moment that suits you. One minute and 10 seconds into your speech is too early to provide a context within which to answer. Five minutes and 45 seconds into your speech leaves you too little time to respond and round off your speech. The best time to accept a point is when you have just completed one of your arguments, enabling you to respond directly and move on with your speech.

It is very important to answer points directly. Failure to engage is something that adjudicators look for. It only takes a moment but can make all the difference in a close debate. One way that some speakers try to get around answering Points of Information is by not accepting any points. Adjudicators are given clear instructions to punish speakers who fail to take two points in their speech. Be warned!

Manner

The rules state: "Manner is the presentation of the speech. It is the style and structure a member uses to further his or her case and persuade the audience." On paper, style and structure account for half of the overall impression upon which adjudicators base their marks. It is, therefore, very important to find out what is considered good style and good structure in Worlds Style debate. In practice, however, my experience on thousands of adjudication panels tells me that style and structure account for a good deal less than half the overall mark.

STYLE

Under style, the rules list as relevant "eye contact, voice modulation, hand gestures, language, the use of notes and any other element which may affect the effectiveness of the presentation of the member." WS lauds eye contact. Changing the tone and volume of your voice and using pauses for emphasis are encouraged. Language should be kept clear and simple—debaters should steer clear of language that is verbose or confusing. Looking down at notes, beyond the occasional glance, detracts from manner.

Style should be appropriate to the subject matter. If you have a sunny, upbeat disposition, use it to inject some much-needed life into a debate about voting reform, for example. In your next debate, about the use of torture as a weapon in the war on terror, it would be advisable to change your tone. Because a debate is artificial—you don't choose which side to speak on based on your genuine beliefs

—it can be easy to forget that you are talking about issues that really matter to some of the audience. An average reasonable person will want to see a connection between your emotional register and the subject under discussion.

Debate is a live event, and audiences enjoy a speaker who can command attention and interest with wit. Jokes work best when they flow naturally from the subject matter and are integrated into a speech. Although debating has attracted some brilliantly funny people, it is not the forum for stand-up comedy, gag after gag. Remember, debaters are asked to talk about some very serious topics, matters of life and death, emotive issues like abortion and eating disorders that will have personal resonance with many people in the room. All style should be appropriate to the subject matter—humor is no exception.

Whenever I ask for a list of great public speakers and communicators, the names Bill Clinton, Barack Obama, Tony Blair, Martin Luther King, Jr., and Ronald Reagan appear somewhere high on the list. What helps these men stand out from the political crowd is their ability to connect with people. Above and beyond the intellectual force of their arguments is an emotional power that appeals. And, let us never forget the role of the adjudicator—to judge from the viewpoint of the average reasonable person.

The average reasonable person is not a debate-consuming robot, motivated only by logic and the buzzwords of social science. He or she is passionate, emotional, moved by feeling and insight. Adjudicators enjoy being moved by speakers who take the trouble to look at them, speak to them intelligibly, use clear language, and communicate fluently without a script.

In reality, some of the most successful debaters of recent years have not lived up to this theory. Speeches are delivered at increasingly high speeds. The language is abstract, specialized, and devoid of power. The average reasonable person would often not have a clue what was going on as debaters natter on about "positive externalities" and "self-actualization." Adjudicators have caved by taking the responsibility on their own shoulders to record and interpret every detail of the debate, piecing together the winner like a logic puzzle. Decisions can take up to two or three hours—and manner is rarely mentioned during these intense discussions.

There are three main reasons for this.

1. **Strategy** Strategically minded teams have come up with ever-more-expansive cases, hoping to prevent the other team from finding new, exciting areas to explore. More arguments in the same amount of time require you to talk faster to squeeze them in. Until adjudicators start deciding that better manner is more important than an additional argument at the margin, the trend will continue.

2. **Globalization** Debating has international competitions every week somewhere in the world. Competitors come from different countries, diverse cultures, and have varied levels of competence in English. As the rule says: "Adjudicators should be aware that at a World Championship, there are many styles which are appropriate, and that they should not discriminate against a member simply because the manner would be deemed 'inappropriate Parliamentary debating' in their own country."

In an effort to be fair, adjudicators have tried to move away from what are seen as subjective style criteria toward supposedly objective matter and structure criteria. It is now common to encounter a new English-as-a-second-language speaker on the debating circuit, speaking at a hundred miles an hour, unintelligibly, trying to live up to the style he sees from the top speakers. It saddens me that efforts to ensure fairness for ESL speakers have led, in effect, to greater exclusion by requiring speed of mouth.

3. **Feedback** It is now customary for adjudicators to give verbal feedback to teams after their debates. This is a chance to tell each team how they could improve, but also a forum to explain their decision. In my experience, worldwide only a handful of adjudicators remain who are prepared to tell a team that style weighed heavily on their decision to place them third or fourth. The back and

forth of argument and rebuttal seem safer ground on which to base a decision.

So what should I do?—I hear you ask. I will be honest. If you want to win Worlds Style debates, as they happen right now, you will sacrifice poetry and pauses for speed and efficiency.

But perhaps the tide will turn. Certainly, when you use your debating skills in the real world, in presentations, meetings, negotiations, advocacy, advice, or any communication situation, the ability to move people as Obama does or King did will be more highly prized. Not even lawyers speak as quickly as debaters. It is a by-product of the design of debate and the cowardice of adjudicators.

Perhaps you will be the one to start to reverse the trend.

STRUCTURE

The first time I attended the Cambridge IV, after a succession of defeats, I summoned up the courage to ask the advice of a much older student who had twice beaten us that day. He gave me one word—*structure*—and then walked off. I thought him very rude, but nevertheless followed his advice and it started to pay dividends. It was both the shortest and most useful conversation about debating I ever had.

Every speech should be structured. Every team should organize its matter across both speeches in the way that maximizes its persuasiveness. You need to be consistent within a speech and across a team. Each speaker must have something new to say (unless you are Closing Government/Opposition). Speeches should have an introduction and conclusion as well as arguments. You need to make sure you make a seven-minute speech. You need to spend time on the most important aspects of what you have to say.

Begin your speech by telling your audience where you are going to take them. The subtlest way to achieve this is to start your speech with an outline of your case that contains the names of your arguments, so that when adjudicators hear them again, they understand where they fit into your case. If you have less faith in the listening skills of your panel, you can choose to signpost—saying, "My points will be a, b, c, and d, before my partner goes on to say e and f."

The simplest way to structure the body of the speech is to divide it into rebuttal and arguments. Equally, you can deal with themes, combining rebuttal and arguments as you go along. If adjudicators understand the outline of your case and the names of the arguments you intend to make, it will make a lot more sense than if you pop them out of nowhere.

One way to highlight your command of structure is to refer to your partner's arguments. In response to a Point of Information, for example, you can give a direct answer, then show how your partner already covered the point. Or, a first speaker can list the intended points of her partner. This gives listeners the impression of clear thinking and control.

Had I been writing this book 10 years ago, I would have suggested that three points is the norm for a seven-minute speech and mentioned the possibility of making two arguments if you have a lot of rebuttal to cover. Certainly some debaters exceeded these guidelines, but their style was thought to be inferior and it limited their success.

Now, very few debaters honor these constraints. By increasing the speed of delivery, they have opened up new possibilities. Four, five, six, or more points in a speech are not uncommon.

With so many ideas to be covered, the importance of structure has never been greater. Linking them together into a story that makes sense and integrating it with your partner's ideas take great ingenuity.

The risk is that you aim for a high target number, trying to use all the possible material, and end up with a few rogue points at the end, forced in with a shoehorn. You are under pressure not to leave arguments for the closing team. But remember that their ideas need not only to be new but also to be important. If you have focused on the heart of the debate for the majority of your time, they can abstract as much as they like or add as many examples as their creativity allows. You will have done well.

Instead, work from your case. If an argument needs to be made to support your story, make it. If it sits outside your case, then focus on deeper analysis of the points you have already offered. I have never heard an adjudicator criticize a team for going into points in too much depth. I would encourage you, despite all the pressures, to aim for quality, not quantity.

One of the most common faults of debaters is underestimating how quickly time passes while they are talking. Worried, perhaps, about running out of things to say, speakers will delay making their final point until the six-minute bang has sounded. This leaves only 60 seconds to make the argument and conclude the speech. Even if adjudicators are able to grasp the point in that time, they are left to form the conclusion, perhaps wrongly, that the speaker didn't think it particularly important.

With practice, you can gain an instinctive sense of the length of a seven-minute speech, but you may still want some help in keeping track of time. You can place a stopwatch on the lectern or table in front of you during the debate. Alternatively, your teammate can time your speech and give you hand signals to show you when each minute is up. Any of these methods can help you apportion sufficient time to all of the areas you want to cover.

Framing and Language

In a debate world where style has been relegated to a tiebreaker, there is still scope for the artful debater to add power to her words through the use of framing and language.

Framing is defining the conceptual building blocks used to construct the debate. *Death tax, pro-life, nuclear and renewables, nanny state, pro-business, corporate handouts, insurgents, terrorists, rebels, collateral damage, independent body*—all these terms carry connotations for good or ill.

If your title is catchy, chances are that people will start using it. So—if you are going to set up an expensive, powerful, unelected commission of bureaucrats, call it an "independent body." If you are going to take action against armed militants, call them "terrorists" rather than "rebels." If you want the government to support companies through the recession, call it "pro-business politics" not "corporate handouts."

If people start using your term, they will begin to think differently about the debate. Ideas will be packaged in ways favorable to your side. Equally, if the other side is framing the debate in a way you don't like, challenge the language. Relabel their points, giving them the meaning you want them to bear:

> *Three times you described our policy as "nanny state." No—our policy is right because we believe in a welfare state, where people in need are looked after, not left to struggle alone.*

This is much better than ending up in a position where you are saying, "Yes, it is a nanny state but what's wrong with that?" The designation is too loaded to accept. It carries emotion that will damage your case, even though it is simply a label.

Framing and language can also go badly wrong. If you label Africa as "a country" and go on and on about it being "tribal," adjudicators will be wincing as they listen to you. If you casually refer to homosexual men as "deviants" and equate gay sex with pedophilia, it will color everything else you say. In short, be aware that language reveals your worldview, just as arguments do. Keep control of your terminology.

Finally, try to avoid using debating buzzwords. If your speech sounds like this:

> *Mr. Speaker, we on Closing Opposition will rebut the status quo case brought by Opening Government and the knife brought by*

Closing Government before extending and adding clash with our own positive matter.

...then you need to spend less time with debaters, get out and meet some new people. These technical terms are useful for understanding debate, training for debate, and thinking about debate. But that does not mean that you should use them in a speech where the aim is to persuade the average reasonable person.

Giving advice on manner is difficult. Nowhere in Worlds Style is there a comparable divide between the rules and how they are implemented.

There are some certainties. Good structure is as important as it ever was. Effective framing and strong labels for your key ideas are crucial.

In the area of style, fashions have changed before and may change again. Currently, successful debaters try to deploy as many arguments as they can within the time available. No consensus has formed among adjudicators that speaking too fast, without pauses, without color can be penalized, despite the written rules to that effect. I am, therefore, torn in my advice. You can choose the path of speed and efficiency or the path of style and beauty. The choice is yours.

3

How to Adjudicate

Imagine going to your first figure skating competition. You have been training on your jumps and rotations, mastering your half lutz and mazurka, and you are feeling confident. The music begins and you perform to the best of your abilities, doing everything you were taught in lessons. Then the judging comes through and the marks are low. Disappointed, you go to ask the three judges for more feedback. You enter the room and it turns out the first judge is someone you recognize, a novice who has attended your skating class for less time than you and wasn't selected for the competition. The second judge, a friend of the woman who runs the rink, has never seen skating before but said she would help out. The third is an experienced skater who had a big fight with your coach five years ago. Are you any less disappointed by your low scores? Have you truly learned anything about your skating skills and abilities?

The biggest criticism of debate adjudication is that—at its worst—it offers debaters experiences like those of our imaginary skater. Anyone who has been debating for a few years will have a story to tell about a debate where the judges got it wrong according to the teams in the room.

But what is remarkable—when you consider how subjective persuasion can be—is not how widespread these tales of injustice are, but how rare. A tiny proportion of the results of competitive debates are officially challenged by debaters. Through a stable body of rules, adjudicator tests, briefings, and feedback over long periods, the debate community has managed to bring the subjective judgments of adjudicators closer together.

One crucial distinction that helps in that regard is that greater technical expertise is needed to recognize a figure skating jump than it does to be the "average reasonable person" of debate rules. And, when all else is stripped away, an adjudicator is just an average reasonable person asking, "Is this persuasive?"

This chapter aims to take you deep into the mind of the adjudicator and shine a light on the deliberations that produce the results. We look at the adjudicator's mindset and how judges overcome biases in themselves and the process to try to get the right result. We also explain how they reach that magic number between 50 and 100 that marks your speech. It is designed for debaters who want to gain an insight into their judges and for adjudicators who want to improve their skills.

Adjudicators

If you attend tournaments, you will find all sorts of people end up as adjudicators: former debaters who have left the university but come back to help out and see old friends; current debaters who were not selected for their teams but want to come and be part of the tournament. You will meet some adjudicators who rarely or never debated themselves but have come to tournaments and devoted their energies to learning how to judge. You will also encounter students from the host institution, many of whom will often be inexperienced. Occasionally, you will be judged by the coaches of other teams.

Organizers will make an effort to create a panel of at least three adjudicators for every round. They will appoint a Chair, who is usually the person they deem the best adjudicator of the three. If a competition is short of judges, occasionally the organizers will put an experienced adjudicator in a room on his or her own.

Once the debate is over, the panel will discuss the result and come to a consensus. If that isn't possible, a vote is taken, with the Chair being the tiebreaker. The Chair is required to give verbal feedback on the debate, explaining the reasons for the panel's decision and offering advice on areas in which you can improve. You can also ask for more detailed feedback afterward—judges are usually more than happy to spend a couple of minutes to help guide you.

To avoid bias, you won't be judged by someone who is a student or the coach of an institution involved in your debate or in a relationship with a debater in your room. If a debater or adjudicator feels there is a conflict, she is asked to report it and the organizers will switch adjudicators.

After the debate, or in the break between rounds, take some time to talk to adjudicators about what bugged them, what amazed them about the best team they saw. If you can, put yourself forward to adjudicate. It is a great learning experience to sit on the other side of the table and realize what is going through the judges' minds when you speak.

Setup

The setup of an adjudication panel follows some basic rules and conventions. A typical preliminary round has three adjudicators. Octo-, quarter- and semifinals may have five adjudicators. A final will often have seven or even nine adjudicators.

One of the adjudicators will be appointed Chair. The Chair is the person referred to by debaters as Mr. or Madam Speaker. Her or his job is to keep order, ensure that the speeches are timed, manage the panel, and fill out the paperwork that records the result. The Chair has the tiebreaking vote—if the panel is equally split, he or she decides the winner.

Other adjudicators (often called "wings," in reference to the convention that the Chair sits in the middle) help form the consensus on which the decision is made. If it comes to a vote, two wings can outvote the Chair. One of the wings will act as timekeeper in addition to his judging responsibilities.

Before the start of the round, the Chair will hand out the ballot paper to the teams so teams can check that they are in the right room and the right position on the table. Each team will also indicate at this stage the order in which they intend to speak (although they can change their mind during the debate).

Having got back the ballot and ensured that one of the judges has assumed responsibility for time keeping, the Chair will introduce the debate, saying something like:

> I call this House to order. Welcome to Round 1 of the Barbaria National Debating Championships 2011. The teams are Namon A in Opening Government, Abalob B in Opening Opposition, Bingchang A in Closing Government, and Habanila C in Closing Opposition. Speeches are seven minutes in length. After one minute, you will hear this sound (bang), which means Points of Information can be offered by the other side. After six minutes, you will the sound again (bang), which means Points can no longer be offered. After seven minutes, you will hear this sound (bang, bang) after which you should draw your speech to a close. The motion before the House is that "This House Would Allow the Sale of Human Organs." I now invite the Prime Minister to open the case for the Government.

At the end of the speech, the Chair will speak again, saying something like:

I thank the speaker for his/her speech and call upon the Leader of the Opposition to open the case for his/her side.

Each speaker should be called by the Chair and thanked for her or his contribution after his or her speech.

The only other interventions the Chair will make in the debate are if someone tries to offer a Point of Information in a speaker's protected time or if a Point is offered legitimately but goes beyond 15 seconds. In these instances, the Chair can say "order" or "out of time" and signal to the offending party that he should sit down. A good Chair should let the debate flow and say as little as possible.

Mindset

How can an adjudicator—with his individual identity, prejudices, preferences, and opinions—judge what is persuasive without being persuaded? Let's look at the peculiar mindset of the adjudicator and start by looking for guidance from the rules. Adjudicators should:

- assess from the viewpoint of the average reasonable person.

- analyze the matter presented and assess its persuasiveness, while disregarding any specialist knowledge they may have on the issue of the debate.

- not allow bias to influence their assessment.

- not discriminate against debaters on the basis of religion, sex, race, color, nationality, sexual preference, age, social status, or disability.

The most important part to get your head around is the "average reasonable person." The average reasonable person is assumed not to have specialist knowledge on the issue of any debate. You may have a PhD in political science, but if a debater gets up and bases his speech on the "veil of ignorance" without explaining what it means or where it comes from, you should not fill in the gaps for him. You might have personal experience of serving in the armed forces, but if a debate gets onto the question of military tactics, however strongly you feel, you need to put those feelings to one side.

When adjudicators do their job well, debaters who study law, economics, or politics are not at an advantage. They have to explain concepts with which they are familiar in a new context, making them accessible to those without their grounding in the subject.

Judges must suspend their opinions without losing the critical faculties that created them. It is a difficult exercise because judges must avoid discrimination and bias. Obviously, an arbitrary hatred of women or men, black people, or Israelis would be a totally unacceptable basis for any decision. Discrimination can sneak in in subtle ways to infect our decision making. In an abortion debate, do we give greater credence to the views of women? In a debate about slavery, do we discount the views of white Europeans? Is a debater who is openly gay treated as an expert on issues around homosexuality? Discrimination on the grounds of identity is not permissible, whether it fits the traditional or the modern mold.

Bias often is more difficult to suppress. Average reasonable people like you and me have opinions. We feel incredibly strongly about some things, sometimes so much so that we are prepared to give up our time to write, lobby, march, campaign, and vote. Even on those issues we care less about, we will have opinions created through a mixture of upbringing, feelings, and reasoned thought. When a new idea comes along—is computer-simulated pornography wrong?—we have an instinctive answer lurking inside us. Not only that but we often have explicitly considered arguments that come up in debates and have rejected them in the process of forming our own opinions.

Let's imagine I am judging a debate on something I have thought about deeply—whether the Alternative Vote (AV) electoral system should be adopted in the UK. The subject of an unprecedented national referendum in 2011, AV involves moving from putting a simple X in the box of your favorite candidate to ranking the candidates in order (1, 2, 3, etc.). This fragment is from the first minute of the Prime Minister's speech.

> *Firstly, the Alternative Vote system should be adopted for British general elections because it is more proportional. Proportional systems are fairer because the number of seats a party receives in Parliament more closely reflects their national share of the vote. It cannot be right that the Liberal Democrats gained almost a million votes at the 2010 election but lost five seats. The votes of those million people should have counted for something.*

When I heard the motion was about voting system reform, I was pleased because I had studied political science and wrote a dissertation on voting and electoral reform. Here's what is going on in the back of my mind, listening to this *without* my adjudicator's hat on, with my unkempt thoughts in brackets.

> *Firstly, the Alternative Vote system should be adopted for British general elections because it is more proportional* [what? You idiot! It isn't more proportional, it just takes account of people's preferences better. Oh no, this debate is going to be terrible now]. *Proportional systems are fairer* [why?] *because the number of seats a party receives in Parliament more closely reflects their national share of the vote* [but that would not necessarily happen under AV!]. *It cannot be right that the Liberal Democrats gained almost a million votes at the 2010 election but lost five seats* [why not? And anyway that or worse could happen under AV!]. *The votes of those million people should have counted for something* [oh no, they've totally got the wrong end of the stick. I wonder if Opposition will call them on it. These guys are going to come in fourth].

Now, while it is sad for me that my pet topic is being massacred, these responses are not the right way to think as a judge. Let's have a go *with* my adjudicator's hat on.

> *Firstly, the Alternative Vote system should be adopted for British general elections* [OK, that's clear] *because it is more*

proportional [that's not true! But would an average reasonable person know that? Probably not. OK, let's see where this goes]. *Proportional systems are fairer because the number of seats a party receives in Parliament more closely reflects their national share of the vote* [fair=share in Parliament. Interesting. I wonder if that will be challenged]. *It cannot be right that the Liberal Democrats gained almost a million votes at the 2010 election but lost five seats* [Because fair=share in Parliament? OK]. *The votes of those million people should have counted for something.*

As an adjudicator, I am slow to draw conclusions. I spend more time understanding points and less time assessing them myself. When the Opposition speaks, I allow them to provide the critique.

I still know that AV is not a proportional system. But it is just possible that this piece of information, though key in academic discussions of various voting systems, will turn out to be irrelevant to the debate. If the Opposition accepts the contention that AV is proportional and argue against AV because they oppose all proportional systems, we could have a good debate, albeit using a misleading label for the issues under discussion. Had I dismissed Opening Government as hopelessly ignorant and automatically fourth, I would be left with nowhere to go when the other teams showed equal ignorance.

Rarely is it appropriate for a judge to make a call between teams on their knowledge base. Yet, teams often spend a lot of time and effort trying to impress adjudicators with the encyclopedic content of their minds. A good example of knowledge one-upmanship I recall was a debate about teaching in foreign languages held in Malaysia. The Opening Government decided, for reasons best known to themselves, to place the debate in Switzerland, where they said there was one official language—French. The Opening Opposition engaged in the debate but not before correcting the Opening Government by disclosing there were two official languages—French and German. Closing Government started by saying—as an aside—that previous teams had overlooked Italian, the third official language of Switzerland. And, finally, Closing Opposition informed me, with a knowing look, that Romansch was a fourth. It was funny but irrelevant to the outcome of the debate.

Adjudicators often find themselves in difficult situations. Suspending what you know in favor of what the average reasonable person knows can take mental dexterity. The tough situations are where a call has to be made. Returning to our Alternative Vote debate, let's assume that the Opposition says this:

> We accept that the UK electoral system should become more proportional. It is for that very reason that we oppose AV. AV is just a different way of calculating who wins in first-past-the-post—ordering the candidates 1, 2, 3 rather than putting a X in the box. It could just as easily create a less proportional result as a more proportional result. The Government's proposal is wrong—and their own argument proves it.

Now I know this explanation to be true. The difficulty I face is that I can't accept it—even though it's right. I must give Government a chance to say how they think their AV system works. They should have done it immediately in the first speech, and I can punish them for failure to define adequately. But I can't just dismiss Government's version the minute I hear the correct version. "Who would I believe if I didn't possess specialist knowledge?" is the question I must ask myself.

This attitude—weighing cases, the quality of arguments, and rebuttal, while taking on board the manner of speakers—is characteristic of adjudication in Worlds Style debate. Judges recognize that objectivity is impossible and try to measure persuasiveness rather than truth. Arguments and rebuttal should be rewarded for their depth, logical exposition, and presentation, not their accordance with the opinions of the panel. The manner of speakers matters because debating should exercise and engage hearts and minds, not check off boxes on a sheet of paper. The adjudicator is not an expert informing debaters of the truth, but an outsider assessing the persuasiveness of their claims.

The Government of What?

Debate is divided into Government and Opposition. But the Government of what? The expansion of debate has led to international competitions held weekly. The issues discussed are global. Adjudicators need to think clearly—taking the motion into account—about whether Opening Government has acted fairly in setting the right forum for the debate.

Armed with the open mind of an average reasonable person, an adjudicator listens closely to the first speaker for her definition. In my AV example, the definition was "the Alternative Vote system should be adopted for British general elections." It doesn't say when or "after a referendum," so it is probably fair to assume, unless it comes up later, that the speaker means immediately and "without a referendum."

This example is from a debate that took place early in 2010 in the UK between teams of law students from London. It was acceptable —in fact, obvious—that they chose the UK as the appropriate parliament for that debate. If a UK team had been visiting Japan and defined the topic as relating only to UK general elections, it would have been unfair.

WS has rules that limit debaters' scope to define the debate. In general terms, a definition must satisfy four requirements. It must:

- be set in the present day
- propose a course of action
- be set in a specific place appropriate to the topic, and
- be fair to the competitors

International debating tournaments and forums make this a difficult task. Ten to 15 years ago, most debates I attended in the UK were defined as relating to the British Parliament: Britain should join the Euro, Britain should legalize drugs, Britain should boycott the Olympics, and so on. Now, very few debates are set in a single country. Debaters prefer to say that all countries should legalize drugs, that the EU countries should legalize drugs, or that all "Western liberal democracies" should legalize drugs. In military debates, occasionally "we" becomes "America" in recognition of its role as global policeman, or "NATO," or "the UN."

Fairness demands that debates involving international speakers should not be tilted in favor of one home country. (The exception at Worlds is the tradition that one motion is about the host nation.) But such evenhandedness has changed the nature of the adjudicator's role in important ways.

First, adjudicators should not penalize a team for proposing a case that supports the status quo in the judge's home country. It used to seen as bad form to run a case, in Opening Government, that supported the status quo. In essence, the Government was proposing to do nothing, forcing the Opposition to come up with a detailed plan and then shooting it down. That is an attractive prospect for any Opening Government team but leads to poor debates and gives the Government an unfair advantage. The worst example of this I recall was at the Durham IV on the day that Australia had voted overwhelmingly to remain a constitutional monarchy in a referendum. In the final, the Opening Government team proposed that Australia should remain a monarchy.

Choosing a more global forum makes such instances less likely. Legalizing assisted suicide across Europe, for example, would change the law in most countries, but not all. Permitting civil partnerships worldwide represents a policy shift for many countries, but, again, not all. As adjudicators, we must not penalize teams for introducing a plan that is the status quo in their home country, if they are intending to roll it out in other countries.

Second, adjudicators should not count heavily arguments that rely on convention. Such arguments are much weaker in an international forum. Let's look at a line from a debate on stem cell research.

> In Europe, we already allow abortion, so we must accept, if the termination of a fetus is permitted, that there are circumstances where it is acceptable to let embryos be destroyed.

The major problem with this argument is that some parts of Europe allow abortion and others do not. To establish that those countries where abortion is still illegal should allow the destruction of embryos in stem cell research requires a different argument. Debaters often gloss over these distinctions in their desire to internationalize debates.

> Gov: "People should be allowed to smoke cannabis in special cafés. They are allowed to smoke tobacco and that is proven to be far more dangerous."

> Opp: "But they can't smoke tobacco in a café in many countries because of secondhand smoke."

This is frustrating. The Government is trying to justify cannabis cafés by reference to existing laws on tobacco. Opposition is trying to oppose cannabis cafés by reference to other tobacco laws. Neither is bothering to establish a principle by which we might judge whether smoking cannabis in special cafés is acceptable. What if the tobacco laws changed? Where would that leave these arguments?

Third, adjudicators should reward teams that try to establish clash and penalize those that hide behind shifting examples. In an internationally based debate, teams need to do more to establish clash. The more broadly defined the territory, the greater the number of potential examples and counter-examples. It will suit each side to choose examples that fit its understanding of the debate. This can be hugely unsatisfactory and difficult to adjudicate.

> Gov: "We believe that constructive engagement is always the right way to proceed. You need to offer a carrot as well as a stick.

Look at Cuba, where America has failed to engage and the Castros still run the island after fifty years."

Opp: "But look at North Korea, where the Americans have given aid, technology, food—they still hate America, they are militarily aggressive, and they have an active nuclear weapons program."

So it's 1–1. If we were discussing a specific country, we could get into a discussion about why constructive engagement sometimes succeeds and sometimes fails, then assess how similar that country was to Cuba/North Korea. But, because we have moved into a general discussion of principle, debaters will keep lining up the examples. Adjudicators must reward speakers who get into the deeper questions and analysis.

Who are "we"? It's a big question. In WS debating, after an incredible decade of internationalization, we are as often the world, or an international organization, as we are a single country. Adjudicators need to be sensitive to this and reward debaters who go beyond trading examples to analyzing underlying reasons.

Recording the Debate

Judges need to record the debate. This doesn't mean filming it nor taking down every word in dictation. It means making sufficient notes to fulfill both of the adjudicator's tasks: making a decision and justifying it. Judges often disagree about who should win and sometimes about what was said in the room. Notes are a helpful guide through those issues, enabling adjudicators to reach a conclusion.

The tools of the trade are a pen, paper, and a stopwatch.

I use one sheet of 8½ × 11 paper divided into eight boxes, four on the left, four on the right, with some space left at the bottom for general comments to be used in my verbal adjudication. I then have a basic code to help me remember what all my notes mean. (R) and an attached line signify rebuttal. I attach numbers to arguments. If a point is undeveloped or unsubstantiated, I write (...) after it. If it is substantiated, I write it down in skeleton form. If it is excellent, I use (!), and if it is terrible I write (?), which I think I borrowed from chess notation. I write responses to Points of Information next to a check mark and make note of the person who asked it (G1 for the Prime Minister and so on). If I have a big question or comment about a point, I will write next to it in capitals, in a box, to distinguish my thoughts from the debaters' comments. Sometimes I write a time (5.55) next to a point to show it wasn't given much prominence or (7.40!) that a speech went on too long. This system, if you can call it that, is just what emerged over time. I never exceed a single sheet of notes because I want to be focused on looking at the speaker as much as possible to assess manner, not looking down at a sheet of paper.

Some judges use several sheets, write in different colors, draw special boxes for Points of Information, connect people's rebuttal to other people's arguments with long lines across the page—there are so many ways you can record your thoughts. The important test is whether you can justify your decision at the end of the debate.

Overcoming Bias

The main obstacle to becoming a good adjudicator is overcoming bias. Here are the three most common structural and human biases of which you need to be aware. The Long Diagonal Bias and Guilt by Association emerge from the four-team format of a Worlds Style debate. Entering the debate is a risk in any format. You need to guard against them all.

THE LONG DIAGONAL BIAS

Human beings are forgetful. Even when we remember the past, we tend to assign less weight to what we heard an hour ago to what we are hearing now. In debating, this contributes to the Long Diagonal Bias. Accordingly, Opening Government, who speak first, may appear to have less residual impact on a debate. Closing Opposition, who speak last, tends to linger in the memory. The design of a Worlds Style debate leaves it open to human error. It is a potential error that adjudicators must overcome.

Several structural reasons tend to give Opening Government a harder job. First, they alone must produce a definition—a plan that works. If any problems emerge with their definition over the hour, it hits them hardest. Second, their arguments are submitted early in the debate, which gives all of Opposition the chance to discredit them. Third, only their second speaker has the opportunity to rebut. Fourth, their only way of interacting with the second half of the debate is through Points of Information, and there is a risk of adjudicators forgetting their contribution.

Closing Opposition enjoys natural advantages. First, they get to hear all three other cases before they show their hand. Second, their first speech is delivered 35 minutes into the debate, allowing ample time for thought and preparation. Third, the scope for finding weaknesses and inconsistencies in a case is greater the longer the debate goes on. Fourth, their second speaker can speak freely with no fear of reply. Fifth, they have the final say and their characterization of the debate is fresh in adjudicators' minds when they confer.

If you ever see a semifinal or final at a major competition, you will notice, after the teams are announced, that a member of each team will go forward to draw the position out of a hat. The team that gets Opening Government will normally look disappointed; the team that picks Closing Opposition is usually delighted.

This strong bias has been confirmed by results in debating competitions. Analysis of preliminary rounds in major tournaments shows that Opening Opposition and Closing Government each win around 25 percent of debates, while Opening Government wins less than 20 percent, and Closing Opposition more than 30 percent.

Sitting down to write this section, I have decided to call this the Long Diagonal Bias. Giving it capital letters makes it look important. Using abstract language makes it sound like a well-tested social phenomenon. The term *long diagonal* is sometimes used by adjudicators to describe the interaction between Opening Government and Closing Opposition, with *short diagonal* describing Opening Opposition and Closing Government, simply because they are joined with diagonal lines on the judge's page. It has all the hallmarks of a phrase that will stick in debaters' minds.

Novice debaters, all of whom speak in the preliminary rounds, commonly prefer to speak during the second half of the debate and will often be better in those positions. They have more time to think of arguments and find fault with some of what the other teams have said. Creating a case well takes skills that need more work over a longer period.

Adjudicators must keep in mind their duty to reward Opening Government for doing their job well. If the Prime Minister has a clear definition, makes an excellent case with exceptional manner, he or she deserves a high mark. If the Deputy Prime Minister deals effectively with the Leader of the Opposition, defends and develops the case, he or she should be rewarded. If together, they have defined the problem, proposed a policy, made principled and practical arguments, examined the likely consequences, it sounds like a comprehensive fulfillment of all they can do. It is no good lauding Opening Government for "setting up a good debate" and then giving the other teams all the credit for building on their work.

Adjudicators must also be mindful that they do not punish Opening Government for mistakes more harshly than they would other teams. "That definition was just crazy, I gave them an automatic fourth" is not an acceptable adjudication. When Opening Opposition launches into their argumentation without explaining where they stand on the big picture, I never hear judges say, "Their case was non-existent, I gave them an automatic fourth." Other teams must earn their right to be placed ahead of Opening

Government, and their mistakes must count against them to the same degree.

In finals and semifinals, the Long Diagonal Bias disappears. I believe—though I cannot prove—it is because novice speakers, who predominantly struggle with Opening Government, are out of the tournament and because finals are judged by the best adjudicators, who recognize and correct this natural bias. Certainly, my experience on panels is that less experienced judges plump for Closing Opposition far more often than experienced judges.

GUILT BY ASSOCIATION

Any team can win any debate.

A team can only perform its role. If it does the best job, it deserves to win. The Guilt by Association trap is activated when an adjudicator is so unconvinced by one half of the Government (or Opposition) that she fails to apply her critical faculties to the other half. The key to avoiding it is a simple question, asked frequently: "What does this team have to do to win?"

A sentence I hear too often on adjudication panels is, "They did as well as they could, but they just couldn't win from that position." The typical scenario is as follows. Opening Government does a terrible job, laying out an unworkable plan, and bringing weak arguments. Opening Opposition destroys the plan, shows up its implausibility, and exposes each of the Government's arguments with glee. At this point, an inexperienced judge reaches the conclusion that Closing Government cannot win the debate, whatever they do, and mentally pencils them in for third place. This is Guilt by Association, and it is poor adjudication.

The time-tested remedy is to return to the simple question: "Who was most persuasive?" I do not believe this means "Who did I agree with at the end of debate?" I can appreciate a brilliant case for consensual incest or neoconservatism without agreeing with it. My personal opinion is not on the line, because it has been suspended for the duration of the debate. No, "who was most persuasive" means "How far would you have moved an average reasonable person toward being convinced?"

If Opening Government were truly dreadful, and Opening Opposition were devastatingly good, then our reasonable person is going to be totally convinced by Opposition at the halfway stage. But, if somehow Closing Government can resurrect some ideas, make hearers think again, come up with nagging doubts—even if our reasonable person ends up siding with Opposition—they will have achieved a great deal given the point at which they started. And, it is possible for them to win the debate.

Adjudicators need to think about debates as comprising four teams, not two. A good Closing Government team will step away from the specific proposal, while taking care never, overtly, to reject it and focus on the principle behind the case in greater depth. They will spend a lot of time attacking the Opposition, demonstrating that weaknesses on both sides muddy the water. If they genuinely do "as well as they could from that position," then they deserve a score in the nineties—an exceptional mark, not to be offered lightly

It is not only possible, but common, that opening and closing teams on the same side take first and fourth place. This can seem odd at first to people accustomed to other styles of debate, where a motion either passes or falls. It is one of the great strengths of WS debate. If you struggle with the idea, try asking yourself, "What does this team have to do to win?" If you can't answer the question, keep asking it until you can.

ENTERING THE DEBATE

Adjudicators are there to assess the debate, not to win it. Many judges are frustrated speakers with their own ideas about how a topic should be addressed. Like an opinionated sports commentator, the adjudicator has an armchair from which the right decisions seem obvious. But this urge must be resisted. When adjudicators do get overexcited and start inwardly nominating areas for debaters to discuss, it is called "Entering the Debate"—something you learn to avoid with time and experience. The adjudicators must not enter the debate—they must not substitute their own view of what the debate should be for the debate that actually takes place.

A phrase you should never hear on an adjudication panel in Worlds Style debate is "I can't believe they didn't make the argument about . . . —it's the killer point."

It follows from everything I have said about the mindset and approach of adjudicators that there is no place for preconceptions. The debate you should judge is the debate that happens, not the debate you wish had happened.

Teams should not be rewarded for making the arguments you want to hear. Your personal preferences are neither here nor there. In fact, if you are sitting there devising the killer points you would utilize, were you taking part, you are not focused on the job of listening to the teams.

Adjudicators do need to think ahead. When Closing Government, for example, stands up, it is worth thinking, "What do they need to do to win?" The answer is something close to "deal well with key issues A and B from the top half of the debate and come up with powerful new arguments." It will not be "they have to talk about new issues C and D." The difference is that A and B have come out of the debate, whereas C and D are creations of the adjudicator's mind. Once an issue is live in the debate, it is absolutely acceptable for the adjudicator to demand that teams focus on it should he or she judge it important. But you can't pick issues out of your own head and assess teams against their ability to second-guess you.

As an adjudicator, I hope this section helps you avoid three common mistakes. Entering the Debate, assigning Guilt by Association, and succumbing to the Long Diagonal Bias are very human failings. It is natural for the arguments you hear to provoke thoughts in your own mind. It is difficult to give credit for defending a case you know makes no sense. It is well established that human beings are most swayed by the last thing they hear.

All are overcome by having a frame of mind that is slow to make judgments. When you hear the label to a well-known argument like "people should be free to choose what to do with their own money," don't take that argument as made until it has been substantiated. When you listen to debaters, ignore the voice that says "How would I deal with this point?" and just see what happens in the debate. Don't write off an entire side because one team has performed poorly—suspend your judgment and be open to persuasion. Don't take at face value Closing Opposition's dismissal or ignoring of Opening Government, but think again about what they said.

Then return to the big questions:

- What was their case?
- How persuasive were they?
- How far would they have moved an average reasonable person toward being convinced?

Deliberation

Let's move from the adjudicator's mindset during the debate to what happens immediately afterward. This process of discussion and decision making is known as deliberation. Deliberation transforms the separate views of the adjudication panel into a single, binding result.

When a debate ends, the Chair will thank all of the speakers and invite them to "cross the floor"—they are then welcome to stand up, leave their seats, and shake hands with their opponents before exiting the room.

Once the debaters have left, the process of deliberation begins. The Chair will normally start by asking other judges if they would like to take a short time, perhaps a minute, to look at their notes.

Personally, I find this period of silence unhelpful—I consider debating to be a live event that should provoke, at its climax, an instant decision. But I am always happy to allow people extra time to mull over what they have heard. If adjudicators are using the time to reconsider the beginning of the debate, then it is doubtless an excellent use of time and may help to overcome the Long Diagonal Bias.

Silent reflection and review over, the Chair should ask the other judges for their 1, 2, 3, 4. If any judge is not certain, then the Chair should try to get some sort of commitment—"Opening Government definitely didn't win" or "It's between the Opposition teams but I'm not sure after that." Often, judges want to get into detailed discussion of the debate or start justifying their placement at this stage. It is important that the Chair—politely but firmly—stop that discussion dead in its tracks.

I also think it important that the Chair refrain from expressing his or her opinion before hearing from the other adjudicators. In competitions, wing judges often fear getting a bad report from a more experienced Chair. A Chair's forceful statement in support of Opening Opposition can leave a wing judge feeling pressured to follow suit. It is more respectful, and more likely to create genuine compromise, if the Chair listens before expressing his or her view.

Having spoken to each of the judges, the Chair will have a sense of where the discussion needs to focus. I note down people's rankings—in no particular order—on a sheet of paper, especially when there are five, seven, or nine on a panel. Let's say we have a five-person panel.

JUDGE	OG	OO	CG	CO
Julia	4			1 or 2
Ahmed	3 or 4	3 or 4	1	2
Jose	4	1	3	2
Belinda	2	1	3 or 4	3 or 4
Me				

Leaving my own judgment to one side, we have a variety of responses to the debate. Had everyone agreed on the winner and second-place team, we could have spent all of our time discussing third and fourth. As it is, we need to consider the whole debate and look at each team in turn.

I would start the discussion by asking Belinda, the biggest fan of Opening Government, to talk us through what she liked about them. Having looked at the pros, I would ask others to introduce the cons, bringing Opening Opposition under consideration. Given that Belinda, Jose, and Julia all think OO outperformed OG, and Ahmed isn't sure, it is likely that they will all come to agreement on this point.

I would then invite Ahmed, Closing Government's most fervent advocate, to highlight what he liked about them. Jose and Belinda would then get the chance to say why they felt Opening Opposition did better. Julia's contribution here will be valuable. In light of the discussion, she will firm up her own opinion and bring us closer to consensus. Having heard the views of others, Ahmed is happy to accept OO as better than OG. Julia has decided that CG were third and OO were either first or second.

Going round the room again, I note:

	OG	OO	CG	CO
Julia	4	1 or 2	3	1 or 2
Ahmed	4	3	1	2
Jose	4	1	3	2
Belinda	2	1	3 or 4	3 or 4
Me				

We now talk about Closing Opposition, with Julia taking the lead. As Chair, I should ensure that Belinda gets plenty of time to talk about her reservations. Having moderated one anothers' positions, we now get to final commitments. As Chair, I will introduce my personal ranking at this stage—the latest possible moment.

	OG	OO	CG	CO
Julia	4	1	3	2
Ahmed	4	3	1	2
Jose	4	1	3	2
Belinda	2	1	4	3
Me	4	1	3	2

At this point, I will suggest that we are heading toward the order:

1	2	3	4
OO	CO	CG	OG

Julia and Jose will happily agree. As it is my preference, we already have enough votes to declare the result. But a good Chair prefers, wherever possible, to reach a consensus and take all the panelists with him or her.

"Is there anything that would persuade you that Opening Government took the fourth, not the second?" I would ask Belinda. "What would make you think Opening Opposition won?" I would put to Ahmed. In addition, if the other adjudicators can go some way to answering their objections, Belinda and Ahmed will feel better about the decision and be able to accept it, even if they don't necessarily share the conviction.

This process may seem very directed. But bear in mind that a panel is normally allowed only 15 minutes to reach a decision. Without focus and structure, the loudest voices will take up all the airtime, and you will end up with a divisive vote rather than an inclusive consensus.

Also, while the Chair is active in the sense of directing discussion, note that his or her opinions do not dominate the panel. The wise Chair avoids revealing any opinions until the last moment, encouraging other judges to come forward with opinions, and holds off declaring a view and then challenging other judges to disagree. Respect is shown for all opinions and the Chair prefers gentle guidance to loud advocacy for one or the other of the teams.

Despite all this, if a vote is needed to determine a final ranking, the Chair should go through in the following order: Which team came first? Who came second? Who came third? Who came fourth? Even if the most extreme position emerges and, on a five-person panel, the winning team has only two votes, with every other team getting one vote, that is enough to declare that team the winner. That team then drops out of consideration for second, third, or fourth.

Having reached a decision, the Chair will fill out the ballot paper, writing 1st, 2nd, 3rd, 4th, and/or 3, 2, 1, 0 in the relevant boxes. But the job is not yet done. At this point, the panel needs to reach agreement on speaker points—the points the individual debaters are awarded for their performance.

In any debate, adjudicators are instructed to ensure that the aggregate of a team's speaker points reflects the position of the team in the debate. So, if a team comes in first, it must have the highest aggregate speaker points. The second-place team must have lower aggregate speaker points than the winning team and a higher aggregate than the third-place team. The fourth-place team must have the lowest aggregate speaker points. This is sometimes expressed in the instruction "no low-point wins!"

Speaker points are less important than team points. On the overall tournament standings, teams are ranked in order of their team points. When teams have the same number of team points, aggregate speaker points are used as a tiebreaker.

TEAM	TEAM POINTS	SPEAKER POINTS	TEAM POSITION
Camford	6	321	1
Newston	5	322	2
Dhalli	5	315	3
Mandor	5	312	4
Abinara	5	308	5

While speaker points are less important, they do matter. On the above tab, note that all the teams from second place to fifth place have five team points. If the tournament were to break to a final now, the top four teams would qualify. Relatively low speaker marks would cost Abinara a place in the final. In addition, a parallel tab is run for the top individual speakers in the competition. The best individual speaker is usually recognized and, at major tournaments like Worlds, the top 10 speakers are given prizes.

Adjudicators owe it to speakers to take care over their marks. Theoretically, Worlds Style operates a 100-point scale for each speech. In fact, speakers are given a mark between 50 and 100. Here is the guidance given by the Chief Adjudicator at the 2010 World Championships (source: World Debating, http://worlddebating. blogspot.com/2009/12/koc-wudc-debating-guide-speaker-scale. html)

100–95: Plausibly one of the best debating speeches ever given, flawless and astonishingly compelling in every regard. It is incredibly difficult to think up satisfactory responses to any of the arguments made.

94–90: Brilliant arguments successfully engage with the main issues in the round. Arguments are very well-explained, always central to the case being advocated, and demand extremely sophisticated responses. The speech is very clear and incredibly compelling. Structure and role fulfillment are executed flawlessly.

89–85: Very good, central arguments engage well with the most important issues on the table and are highly compelling; sophisticated responses would be required to refute them. Delivery is clear and very persuasive. Role fulfillment and structure probably flawless.

84–80: Relevant and pertinent arguments address key issues in the round with sufficient explanation. The speech is clear in almost its entirety and holds one's attention persuasively. Role is well-fulfilled and structure is unlikely to be problematic.

79–75: Arguments are almost exclusively relevant, and frequently persuasive. Occasionally, but not often, the speaker may slip into: i) deficits in explanation, ii) simplistic argumentation vulnerable to competent responses, or iii) peripheral or irrelevant arguments. The speaker holds one's attention, provides clear structure, and successfully fulfills his basic role on the table.

74–70: Arguments are generally relevant, and some explanation of them given, but there may be obvious gaps in logic, multiple points of peripheral or irrelevant material, and simplistic argumentation. The speaker mostly holds the audience's attention and is usually clear, but rarely compelling, and may sometimes be difficult to follow. There is a decent but incomplete attempt to fulfill one's role on the table, and structure may be imperfectly delivered.

69–65: Relevant arguments are frequently made, but with very rudimentary explanation. The speaker is clear enough to be understood the vast majority of the time, but this may be difficult and/or unrewarding. Structure poor; poor attempt to fulfill role.

64–60: The speaker is often relevant, but rarely makes full arguments. Frequently unclear and confusing; really problematic structure/lack thereof; some awareness of role.

59–55: The speech rarely makes relevant claims, only occasionally formulated as arguments. Hard to follow, little/no structure; no evident awareness of role.

54–50: Content is almost never relevant, and is both confusing and confused. No structure or fulfillment of role is, in any meaningful sense, provided.

This is very detailed guidance. For a simpler rule of thumb:

90+—a Worlds finalist speaking at his or her best
80–89—a speech you would expect to see in the Worlds octo-finals
70–79—average for Worlds
60–69—poor
50–59—reserved for extremely flawed speeches

I concede this is only helpful if you have experience of Worlds! A 72 in one tournament should get a 72 in any other tournament. The more debates you attend, the bigger the bank of speeches you build up, the easier it is to draw comparisons and identify the right score.

The Chair will usually be more directive in setting speaker marks, as he or she tends to be the most experienced adjudicator. The best way to avoid mistakes is to start with the winning team. In our debate, Opening Opposition won, deserved scores around 80–85, and the judges felt the first speaker was better, so the Chair will ask "85?", "84?", "83?" for each speaker until a quick consensus of nods emerges. Closing Opposition came second and it was a very close decision, so you would expect the speaker scores to reflect that—in fact, two judges thought they were better than Opening Opposition when the discussion began. In fact, given the closeness of the discussion, the Chair will insist that the gap between all the teams should not be too wide.

Adjudicators should be encouraged to use the whole scale, between 50 and 100, if the speeches merit it. At times, judges like to play it safe, giving everybody a score between 70 and 80. This is wrong. Sometimes speeches are really good or really bad. Often these speeches will coexist in the same debate. If the adjudicators all agreed that a big gap was evident between one team and another, they have no reason to give the teams similar marks.

Some adjudicators artificially deflate speaker marks at the top end. A worrying number of judges take great pride in parsimony when judging the top rooms—those containing the best teams—at a tournament. As far as I can discern, this stems from a feeling of intellectual superiority and an unwillingness to be impressed by lesser talents. Despite telling adjudicators at Worlds, every year, that excellent speeches should score around 90, very few speeches by excellent debaters are awarded a 90. The average score for a top 10 speaker hovers in the mid-eighties. Great speeches deserve high marks. There is nothing to be gained by failing to recognize excellence.

Once the Chair has filled in the team points and speaker points, the ballot is taken by a runner to the tab room, where the results will entered into the tab—the formal record of results across a tournament. The debaters are invited back into the room and nervously take their seats for the verbal adjudication.

Verbal Adjudication

The Chair's final duty is to tell the teams the result, explain the decision, and offer advice on how the teams can improve.

The best explanations and advice are *constructive* and *specific*. When you talk about each team, start by praising them for what they did well. Try to articulate their case at its strongest to show you understood what they wanted to achieve. Only then go on to show why—in light of the efforts of other teams—they ended in a particular position. Consider:

> *Closing Opposition. I felt there was a slight lack of structure and not quite enough engagement with some of the points coming out*

of Government. You had a few timing issues and didn't prioritize your big points as much as you could have. Manner-wise you were fine, but it was just those problems that meant you didn't have the impact on the debate you might have.

This is like a cold reading, performed by a phony psychic. It could plausibly apply to any speech given at a debating competition. Hiding behind "slight," "not quite," "a few," "some," it is pretending to be nice but the result is that it is too general to be genuinely helpful.

Compare:

Closing Opposition. Your manner was good. You did well to identify that consequences were a big issue and came up with an interesting case about the future for Iran and Syria. But your speeches focused almost entirely on this new material. You basically ignored the Closing Government's case about UN reform. Also, within your case, you seemed much happier talking about Iran, which you did for about eight minutes, than Syria, to which you devoted a minute. In the future, you need to engage with other teams, say what you think about their ideas, and earn the right to talk about your case by explaining how it fits into the debate.

This segment contains the same information about engagement, structure, timing, and manner. The difference is that it highlights strengths first, is specific about weaknesses, and concludes by telling the speakers how they can improve. It is constructive and specific. It is much more useful feedback.

The tone of a verbal adjudication should be kind but honest. If there was disagreement over the decision, I think the Chair should say so—"We did start with very different results, but over the course of the discussion we came to an agreement," or "We were split between two teams and ended up with a vote." So long as you don't name names and end up with members of the panel being scowled at as you talk, debaters benefit from getting a sense of how close the call was.

If you have to give negative feedback, you can be candid without being rude. As an overview, you might say: "Thank you all for your speeches. We did feel this was a poor debate—but within it there were some really good points we witnessed and you can learn a lot from this experience for future rounds." To a debater who let his partner down, you might say: "We have to judge you as a team, and, while the case started really strongly, as the debate went on you conceded more and more ground to the Opposition."

Remember that verbal adjudication is an explanation of your decision, not a justification of your decision. Debaters are supposed to listen in silence, saving any questions for the individual feedback portion of the adjudication. If you are challenged on the grounds that "that's not what we said" or "I was talking about something else," don't feel bad. The answer is that it is the job of a speaker to communicate with the adjudication panel, audibly, clearly, and persuasively. If you didn't understand because they spoke too quickly, quietly, or unclearly, it is their problem—your advice should be that they slow down, speak up, and speak more clearly in future rounds.

In the rare instance when a Chair is "rolled"—that is, outvoted by the wing judges—the Chair can normally choose whether to deliver the verbal adjudication her- or himself or nominate one of the majority wing judges to do so. (I always do it myself—I believe that the Chair is bound by collective responsibility for the decision of the panel.) There are also times where a Chair will strongly disagree with a minor placing, and then there is no escape. Occasionally, a Chair has to tell one team they lost to another, when you fervently believe they did not. My way around this is to say, "The panel felt/believed" when I am giving the collective position—I don't accept it myself. I might add, as an example, "Not everyone felt you gave enough prominence to your excellent Syria point; in the future, ensure that you highlight key points so that judges have no choice but to reward them." I think this communicates the truth in a constructive way without compromising my integrity or naming names.

Verbal adjudication should take between 5 and 10 minutes. Once the Chair is done, he or she should thank the teams and offer to give individual feedback. Some teams take you up on this, others don't.

It is also acceptable, after the verbal adjudication, for wing judges to talk to teams about the decision and offer their own feedback. If you are a wing, and you agreed with the decision, make sure you give that impression when talking to teams. It can be tempting to suggest that you thought more favorably of any given team than the consensus. If you disagreed with the decision, try not to focus on the strength you saw (but others didn't), but how a team could put that strength across better and other areas they can improve further. Whatever your views, make sure you don't give out speaker points. Debaters have been known to use a combination of generous flattery and gentle threats to get these prized numbers out of an adjudicator. Once they do, word spreads quickly. The Chief Adjudicator will find out and will not be pleased. The rules are clear—speakers should not be told their speaker points until the end of the tournament.

Finally, note that many tournaments ask the Chair not to offer verbal adjudication after the last one or two preliminary rounds, so that debaters are unable to work out who has made it to the knock-out rounds—normally called "breaking" or "making the break." Thus, all adjudicators are barred from giving out any details of the result to anyone, even friends or adjudicators in other rooms. Again, a rumor is very easy to trace. Check with the tournament organizers if you are unsure what to do and what you are allowed to say.

Adjudication and ESL

Debaters who speak English as a second language should be judged in exactly the same way as native speakers of English. Whatever their language status, in debates they line up together and compete on an equal basis. At some tournaments, once the preliminary rounds are over, the highest-ranked ESL teams will break to special quarterfinals, semifinals or a final, in recognition of the unique challenge faced by nonnative speakers. Until that point, though, there should be absolutely no difference in treatment.

While it is not unusual for ESL speakers to best native English speakers in debates, rarely do ESL speakers win tournaments or top speaker tabs at competitions where both are present. With even intermediate spoken English, creating a case and forming arguments are possible. With good aural English, debaters should be able to follow a speech and understand the salient points, allowing them to rebut. The type of language encouraged in rules is "clear and simple" not "verbose or confusing," so speakers are encouraged to steer away from the verbal flights that are possible to an articulate native speaker.

I have come across a handful of speakers whose English was unintelligible to me. Try as I might, I could not understand what they wanted to say, except for an odd word or two. In these very rare instances, I have been forced to give a low mark. If you cannot understand what is being said, you cannot reward it. You cannot imagine what you heard and judge accordingly, just as a native speaker who whispered inaudibly would be strongly penalized. I repeat—this is an extremely rare occurrence. Yet the perception among ESL speakers can be that they are being punished for poor style in top-level debates. In my opinion, this is only partly true.

So, what part is true? Some of the time, ESL speakers are being penalized for speaking too slowly. It is never expressed in this way, but because a little extra time (even a small amount) is required to get an idea across when you are searching for the right words, it can mean you make one fewer argument, engage in one fewer piece of rebuttal, cut short one "even if..." argument. When everyone is doing the basics well, these marginal differences count.

By rewarding speakers too highly for the number of arguments, adjudicators can unwittingly put ESL speakers at a disadvantage. Wise to this, some ESL speakers have started trying to keep up with the ferocious pace of their counterparts who have English as their mother tongue. Few can manage it. For the rest, what they gain in number of arguments, they lose in quality of exposition

I believe the single biggest innovation WS could make to help ESL speakers compete equally is a counterintuitive one: Reverse the stealthy downgrading of style as a criterion in adjudication. Talking quickly, with no pauses, no emphasis, no connection, should be penalized by adjudicators. The rules are clear—good style never meant blinding people with obscure words or showing off your vocabulary. When speakers are judged on the clarity and persuasiveness of their style—as well as on the substance of their arguments—the playing field will be leveled for all debaters.

Adjudicators who speak English as a second language should judge in exactly the same way as native speakers of English. The task is to assess the debate on the basis of which team were most persuasive to you—focus on arguments rather than presentation.

I have sat alongside ESL adjudicators who are total novices and ESL adjudicators who are among the finest judges of debate in the world. Even the term *ESL adjudicator* makes me uncomfortable—please understand that no distinction is made between adjudicators on the basis of language. In using the term, I am talking about adjudicators who just happen to speak English as a second language. Knowing that ESL adjudicators judge major finals should be a great incentive for you to become involved in judging with confidence.

If you are asked to judge a debate and feel you haven't kept up, it is natural to feel under pressure or even a little embarrassed. You shouldn't be. The speakers must take their panel as they find them and are responsible for making themselves understood. If an adjudicator can't follow a debater's language, the debater is at fault. If the speed at which a debater speaks makes following the reasoning hard for an ESL adjudicator, again, the debater is at fault.

In an ideal world, all adjudicators would understand everything that all debaters said. But even the most aurally gifted native speaker has a limit to what he can take in. Average reasonable people do not always listen to, let alone follow, boring speeches. By trying to understand a speaker, you are doing all that can be asked of you. Please don't reward a point because you think it sounded good. If you can't explain why it's a good point, the speakers have failed to persuade you.

This section should reassure. ESL speakers and adjudicators should be treated exactly the same as native speakers and adjudicators. Major tournaments offer special ESL finals, but if we were to restore style to its rightful place, many more ESL speakers would win tournaments outright.

Analysis Debates

An analysis debate is a debate that discusses the truth of a proposition, rather than the desirability of a course of action.

In the last few years, Chief Adjudicators at some major tournaments have set one motion that asks debaters to do something different from the norm. Rather than coming up with a definition that proposes taking action, in these debates, Opening Government is expected to argue that the motion is true. The other teams are also supposed to address this question of truth.

When a Chief Adjudicator sets an analysis debate, he or she announces the fact to debaters.

Here are some examples of analysis debate motions:

- This House Believes Iraq Is Better Off Now Than Before the War
- This House Believes Feminism Has Damaged Motherhood
- This House Believes Israel Is Not a Democracy
- This House Believes the Welfare State Has Hurt the Poor

Let's take the last motion. The traditional way of addressing that topic would be to propose welfare reform of some kind, justifying it primarily by its beneficial effects on the poorest people. An analysis debate asks Opening Government to make the case that the welfare state has hurt the poor and leave it at that. Both Opposition teams and Closing Government have the same task: analyze more, analyze better.

Analysis debates are notoriously difficult for adjudicators. They require an extraordinary amount of knowledge on the part of the judges. Consider the Iraq debate. Debaters are forced to make such detailed claims about the current state of affairs in Iraq that the average reasonable person would not be expected to have gleaned from readily available sources. How is the adjudicator supposed to say who is right and wrong on these questions of fact? In traditional debates, these claims and counter-claims are just one weapon alongside normative arguments (which require no knowledge) and predictions of the future (which are not wholly dependent on knowledge). Here they are the whole debate.

The best basis for adjudication when you don't have the knowledge to decide is to focus on those facts that are agreed upon by both sides. If Government and Opposition both accept that feminists have created an expectation that women should work—whether you agree with that historically or not—then the two sides have moved to fruitful ground for assessing whether more women working longer hours has been good for the institution of motherhood. Without such shared facts, adjudicators can find themselves really struggling. With these facts, you can bring your analytical skills to bear.

4

Entering Competitions

Reading two mammoth sections on how to speak and how to adjudicate will not make you a better speaker or adjudicator. "Why didn't you tell me an hour ago?" I hear you ask. Well, I hope the approaches and examples given will be useful to you in making sense of your debating experiences and for avoiding all the mistakes I and others made as we learned to debate.

But really, the fastest way to learn is to do. This section is about entering debating competitions. It lays out what competitions are like and how to get the most out of them.

What Competitions Are Like

Before you show up at a tournament, make sure you pre-register. Debating competitions are often over-subscribed. They will normally have a website to help guide you through the registration process.

When you arrive at the tournament, you will have to register, pay any entry fee, and give your team names. Usually, at intervarsity competitions, your name will be that of your institution followed by a letter, from A onward, depending on the number of teams your institution is entering. At open tournaments, you can be as creative as you want with names, and bounds of taste are frequently breached. Some tournaments have a cap on teams per institution—check before you arrive; with others, the sky is the limit. Similarly, some tournaments operate the N-1 rule. This strange-sounding regulation requires each institution to bring adjudicators—one fewer than the number of teams entered. Thus, if you have two teams, you need one adjudicator. Again, checking beforehand is a good idea. It may cause disappointment if your B team is asked to adjudicate. But if you don't bring a judge and the N-1 rule applies, that's how they will spend their weekend.

At registration, you will normally get a schedule, a map, and details of where you are staying overnight if it is a weekend tournament. After registration, everyone is sent to a hall or lecture theater and the briefings begin—usually one for speakers and one for adjudicators, though these are sometimes combined. The briefings are your big chance to find out how to do well at the tournament. The Chief Adjudicator will run through the rules, lay out his or her interpretation on a few points, the number of rounds, length of speeches, and other key information. You can ask questions at a briefing, so if you are unsure about any of the rules, it is the perfect time to seek clarity. Everyone in the room either is a novice or was at some time, so don't be embarrassed that your question is too basic—if you don't know something, ask.

Before the first round is announced, roll will be called to ensure that all teams and adjudicators are present. This can take a while, particularly if there are absentees. If teams don't show, they need to be replaced by swing teams, sometimes known as dummy teams, of substitute speakers from the home institution, to make the numbers work—there must be a multiple of four.

Once everyone is ready, the positions—the draw—are displayed or announced. The first round is conventionally drawn at random. Normally, the draw appears on a PowerPoint presentation. When you see your team name, look for your position (Opening Government, Opening Opposition, Closing Government, Closing

Opposition) and the room number. If you are an adjudicator, check your room number and the name of your Chair—it will be the first name that appears on the list of adjudicators for that room.

Finally, once everyone knows where they are going, the motion is displayed and announced, then the mad rush begins. You have 15 minutes to prepare—during which you also have to find your room, which could be on the other side of a university campus.

When you arrive at your room, only the Opening Government team is allowed to enter—to give them privacy as they prepare. Other teams must find a quiet spot nearby, usually a table in a corridor or an empty stairwell. Two minutes before the round begins, you will be invited in, told where to sit, and the Chair will take it from there.

Between the debate ending and the result being announced, debaters, having left the room, usually go over parts of the debate and predict the likely result. This is a nervous time, full of "what ifs" and "maybes." Then, you are all called in to hear the verbal adjudication. Knowing the result, and the justification, you can try to grab a chat with the Chair on the walk back to the main hall. He or she may have valuable advice.

This cycle of adrenalin surges continues throughout the tournament. You get the lows of waiting for a round to be announced, followed by the rush of the debate, culminating in the anxious delay before the result gives you closure and you start over again. Nerves and tension are on display. Some people get quite animated, perhaps a little obsessive, about results, while others will zone out.

Make sure you attend all the preliminary rounds. Losing a round doesn't mean that's the end. Tournaments are not run on a knockout basis until the final rounds. In subsequent rounds, you will come up against debaters who have the same (or almost the same) number of team points as you. If the first round was tough, treat it as a learning experience and take comfort from the fact that all your next competitors will be teams that came in fourth in round one. It should get easier.

Between debates, you'll have plenty of time to meet and get to know new people. If you are in a new city and want to take time to see the sights, there is usually every opportunity. If you want to obsess over results and swap stories about crazy things said in debates, you will find plenty of willing souls. Debating tournaments normally run exceptional social events. Debaters often develop close and long-lasting friendships with people they meet at tournaments. There is every reason to anticipate you will have a good time.

When the preliminary rounds end, it is time for the break—the moment of truth when the best teams go through to the knock-out stage. Unless you are extraordinarily gifted, at your first tournament, this will be the end of your involvement as a speaker. Depending on the size of the competition, the top 32, 16, 8, or 4 teams will go through to the knock-out stage, known as the break rounds. In a break round, the top two teams from each debate progress to the next. In the final, one team wins.

If you don't make it to a semifinal or final, you can gain much from watching the best teams take each other on. They are going to showcase skills you hope to develop. Without a doubt, you will hear speakers who inspire you and spur you on to improve. By seeing the best and analyzing what they do, you can learn a great deal.

After the final, prizes are given out—to the winners, to the best speaker, sometimes to the best novice team. If that's you, your team might garner an unexpected trophy to take home.

Selecting Teams and Adjudicators

Choosing who should speak together is an important part of the preparation for a tournament and of managing a debate club. This section discusses approaches you can use to find the right combinations and try, as far as is possible, to keep everyone happy.

The quickest way to make enemies in a debate club is to take on responsibility for team selection! Everyone has a theory for why certain individuals should speak together. A complex, inextricable web of friendships, egos, slights, dislikes, and ambitions can lie behind these theories. As a team activity, the success of each individual depends partly on his or her partner, so strong preferences are common.

Let's look at the pros and cons of a few different approaches.

BEST TO WORST

If you put the best two speakers in your club on the same team, they should have the greatest chance of success. By competing in tougher rooms, against better opposition, they will gain valuable experience and understand what is needed to raise their performance to the next level. If that knowledge and expertise are fed back into the club—informally and at training sessions—then such pairings can benefit everybody. Just one team reaching a semifinal or final can act as a motivator to others within the club and encourage new members to get involved in debating. It can also signal to university authorities that the good name of their institution can be enhanced by supporting debate.

A good team doing well can raise the overall standard if an effective training program is in place where they share their insights. The best speakers must be willing to share what they do well. If this doesn't happen, less successful speakers are worse off under this approach—they are less likely, through strong results, to gain the opportunity to speak in a room that lifts their horizons. Under such circumstances, they may lose motivation and feel that they will never be good enough. Another negative, if resources are scarce, is that while the best two speakers get frequent opportunities, people with less experience may have difficulty getting to tournaments at all.

I recommend a "best-to-worst" selection policy for new clubs trying to build knowledge and make a name for themselves at tournaments. But it must be carefully managed to avoid division. Experiences in top rooms, against the best teams, are precious and should not be sacrificed in the interests of "fairness" within a club; they should be shared systematically with all members to raise the overall level. And you may want to designate some tournaments as training tournaments, specifically excluding your most accomplished speakers from eligibility for selection.

PRO-AM

A term borrowed from the world of golf, *Pro-Am* stands for Professional–Amateur and refers to competitions that pair a top golfer with someone of lesser skill. Thankfully, there are no paid debaters, so experience, rather than money, is the dividing line. A Pro-Am selection policy has team formation pairing your most experienced debaters with the least experienced debaters.

The advantage of this pairing policy is that it gives newer speakers the chance to learn from their more experienced partner. How does she get ready for the debate? What questions does he ask in preparation time? How does she avoid weaknesses in her case? Even before a word is uttered in the debate, so much can be learned through preparing together.

The downsides are that the stronger speaker may—consciously or unconsciously—change her approach to compensate for her partner. She may choose always to speak first, to ensure a strong foundation is in place; she may try to squeeze more points into her speech, ensuring they get across. Any number of these bad habits may develop. The weaker speaker may feel bad about letting his partner down—or be very uncomfortable about being the worst speaker in every room if the gap between the two of them is wide.

In short, the characters of those involved determine whether a Pro-Am team will work. Aware of the downsides, in Scotland, an annual tournament is held where all the teams are so composed, thus the incentives for the stronger speaker to help the weaker are reinforced.

SPECIALIST SPEAKERS

Some debaters would rather cut out their own tongue than speak in the Prime Minister's position. Some love to summarize, drawing the themes of the debate together reflectively. Others naturally generate new arguments and ideas and love to speak third rather than fourth.

Every role on the table is subtly distinct. It follows, therefore, that you need to adapt to your role to perform well in a debate. A team comprising two people who cannot lay out a good definition and solid case will struggle in Opening Government, however well they do during the rest of the day. A team with two summarizers may find it hard to fulfill their charge, in Closing Government and Closing Opposition, to come up with a case that is new, interesting, and important.

You can respond in two ways. The first is to say that a debater should be an all-rounder, able to excel everywhere and adapt to any situation. If you believe this, you will tell your debaters to overcome their reticence and try to improve their abilities in those positions they dislike. The second is to accommodate these natural preferences (and strengths) by teaming up your speakers in a way that takes preferences into account.

In a new club, I would try to avoid people self-defining in this way. It can be used as an excuse for laziness and a reason to stop learning. But, where you have a lot of competition for few places, it can be a useful tiebreaker. A more versatile speaker will be of greater value and so her preferences (and her strengths) are relevant grounds for selection.

CHARACTER-BASED SELECTION

Jan is an outwardly confident, talkative, and decisive person who likes the big picture and wants to get things done quickly. Chris is quiet, a good listener, who likes to weigh up all views in detail before coming down strongly on a position. Would they make a good team?

Some coaches and selectors think they can organize teams by considering the characters of their debaters. In the best scenario, Jan would take the lead in preparation time, coming up with a definition and case and sketching out arguments very quickly; Chris would then point out flaws, suggest corrections, and flesh out arguments. Working collaboratively, they would create a strong case.

That depends. Jan's ideas might be of very poor quality. Jan might be very wedded to those ideas. Chris might, once her observations have been rejected, prefer peace to a prolonged argument with Jan. When the team comes in fourth and the adjudicators criticize them for a poor case with insufficient detail, Jan might tell everyone within hearing that Chris is supposed to be the detail person and she's not working out as a partner.

Predicting how people will work together is very difficult—truly an art, not a science. The unlikeliest combinations have been brilliantly successful, including teams who shared a very deep mutual loathing outside of debates. Other "dream teams," close friends widely predicted to win tournaments, have been mysteriously unable to jell.

I would advise selecting on character only in extreme circumstances. Personality-based predictions of success in debating have a poor record. Avoid pairing speakers by character unless a deep and enduring dislike exists between them and they refuse to speak together.

REGULARS OR ROTATION

Another dimension to the selection question, however you resolve it, is whether to pursue your chosen course consistently over time. Long-term partnerships will often use tournaments as stepping-stones for a more distant journey. So, if you know that a team will be going to Worlds in December, you might offer them opportunities to speak together at tournaments in October and November. This chance may let them develop an understanding, find areas where their approach and knowledge are not complementary and need further work, build confidence in each other, and can help the team to improve in time for the big challenge of Worlds.

Repeatedly speaking with the same partner does not always work out well, however. It can cement weaknesses—for example, if one speaker says he cannot speak first and therefore never learns. The advantages of getting to know each other's minds can become a weakness, if you need a fresh approach and all you have is "team-think" (a mild form of "groupthink"). Rotation forces each debater to learn from speaking with various individuals, all of whom have their own approaches, strengths, weaknesses, and foibles.

I think both approaches have merit, and would not make rotation or regularity the governing principle by which selection is made. But some clubs do put a high premium on one or the other.

HOW TO PICK TEAMS—TRIALS OR SELECTION

Finally, after all the permutations of who speaks best with whom, you still need to decide on a process by which to figure out who you should send and in what combination.

As the individual or committee choosing teams, you can consider your overall impression of debaters during training, internal debates, and other competitions, and then apply your criteria to that. Let's say you want to select on a "best-to-worst" basis. Perhaps Mina has really impressed you in practice and you want to team her up with Pat, who is better on paper but has dipped recently. Your overall impression would be a good guide.

The big alternative is to hold trials. On a particular day, you invite people to come and speak, making your decision based on the performances you see on that day—nothing more and nothing less. Many clubs choose their teams for major tournaments using trials, sometimes with adjudicators invited from other societies to help ensure that they are totally independent. Trials are highly pressured, which creates conditions like a real tournament, and they may seem a more scientific way to differentiate between candidates.

But trials are not a simple solution. You need to decide whether individuals will debate in the same team throughout the trials or rotate. Do you assign individuals to a team or do they self-select? If rotating, who decides and how? Then you need to hold enough debates so that everyone gets a chance in different positions. If someone dislikes the Prime Minister position and yet is assigned it in a trial, she may have difficulty performing effectively. The competitive nature of the trial may cut down on teamwork and leave second speakers at a disadvantage, as their partners may have less incentive to share information with them.

Once you realize how fractious the whole business of selection can be, you might well choose to steer clear. If no great competition for places exists, you may find that allowing debaters to form teams themselves is workable. Even if you are over-subscribed, you could pre-announce that anyone who wants to attend a given tournament should email you their team name and members after, say, 3:00 on Wednesday—and that you will select four teams on a first-come-first-served basis. Or, you could set a deadline for teams and members and then draw the top four at random.

Attractive as it might be to duck the responsibility, what will happen if your best speakers are not selected?; if the random draw selects six males and rejects four females?; if one of your members consistently cannot find a partner? Leaving it to chance can present as many new problems as the old ones it solves.

I recommend selection based on observations over time, rather than the examination conditions created by a trial. It is tempting to say that a one-day event is fairer, but the small number of debates and large number of variables bring that into question.

Post-Tournament—Getting the Most Out of It

Everyone comes back from a tournament with stories to tell. Great speeches, social events, remarkable characters, unbelievable gaffes, adjudicator decisions—all provide fuel for the jaw.

Much of this debating gossip is entertaining and, by conveying a sense of enjoyment, can motivate others to want to take part in competitions. When I started out at the University of Leeds, we had to write a short paper on each tournament attended and report back to the society that week. Because we had not won a competition in 115 years, a premium was put on being witty, describing moments of embarrassment, and detailing, in full, who did what at the socials.

Unfortunately, we spent less time relating what we had learned. In those days, tournaments had no verbal adjudication after debates and no standardized tabulation system, so determining why you had won or lost your rounds was not possible. Sometimes all you knew was that you hadn't come in first. Now there is no excuse.

Debaters should make brief notes—What was their case, what happened in the debate, and what did the adjudicators say? By making this information available to the rest of the club as a short presentation or by building up a file, debaters can ensure that the lessons learned also help others within their debating society. Perhaps the A team was told in round 3 that they hadn't provided enough new material—reviewing that decision can help others gain an appreciation of how to approach the role of third speaker.

Unless you are part of a well-established, open, thriving, and hugely successful debating society, the largest part of skill development will come from competitions. Not everyone can go to competitions. Therefore, you need to make a strong effort to establish protocols by which the lessons learned at debating tournaments are passed on to others. Training—formal and informal—should be rewarded within your club if you want to improve quickly, to attract new members, and to keep them.

ESL

Many debaters speak English as a second language. Some tournaments, especially the larger ones, recognize an English as a Second Language champion alongside an overall champion. Worlds also has an English as a Foreign Language category for those with a lower level of facility with English.

Different rules govern both eligibility and how you become ESL or EFL champion. If you are attending a tournament and English is not your first language, you will usually be asked to say whether you meet that tournament's criteria for inclusion. Among the questions officials may ask: Do you study in English? Have you lived in an English-speaking country and for how long? Have you previously moved to elimination rounds in a major tournament? If they determine that your proficiency in English enables you to compete on an equal basis, then you may not be classified as ESL. Note that rules differ between tournaments—you may be ESL at one, but not at another.

As an ESL speaker or team, you will compete on an equal footing with other teams in the tournament during the preliminary rounds. Then it gets complicated. If you make the main break, congratulations! You will then progress to the knock-out rounds. But you will also have made the ESL break, thus becoming eligible for the ESL knock-out rounds. Some competitions will deem you ineligible for the ESL break because you made the main break, others will let you compete in both.

In those ESL knock-out rounds—at Worlds the break is to quarterfinals, at other tournaments to semifinals or just a final—the adjudicators pick the best two teams from each debate to progress until only four teams remain to compete in the final. Once you get to the final, adjudicators select only the winning team.

That's how to win as a team. But you can also be chosen as the best individual ESL speaker. There is more complication here. Some tournaments only designate whole teams as ESL—thus, you are ESL if both team members meet the ESL criteria. Other tournaments allow an individual speaker to count as ESL, making her or him eligible to win individual ESL speaker prizes even if paired with a native English speaker and the team did not advance to the ESL knock-out stages. So, a speaker who didn't make the ESL break could end up the winner of the best ESL speaker prize.

If you are confused, imagine how it felt sitting on the committees that thought up these rules. The prime rule is to check in advance:

- Do they have an ESL break?
- What are the ESL eligibility criteria?
- Are only teams ESL-eligible or individuals also?
- What awards are on offer for ESL debaters?

Remember that ESL speakers are always welcomed at any competition on an equal footing. But, if you are interested in the additional recognition offered by an ESL break, then you must do your research. Check the website, contact the convenor of the tournament, and ask.

Even if you don't reach the ESL final, make sure you watch it. Debating in a second language certainly poses challenges. Invest an hour of your time to see, in action, those who are best able to overcome them.

5

Holding Competitions

Hosting tournaments is a tried-and-tested way to develop a thriving debate club. By attending tournaments, you can send a few students to other societies to pick up tips and return with them. By hosting a tournament, you can bring hundreds of students and adjudicators directly to your school. Wherever Worlds Style debate has taken root, it has grown around new institutions holding competitions that attract established institutions and competitors.

The most recent hosts of Worlds were Botswana and Turkey. Neither is a traditional debating powerhouse, but, for both, Worlds was the culmination of a long process. Over several years, on the path toward holding Worlds, they hosted competitions as an integral part of their strategy to develop debate.

This section advises you how to run an excellent tournament. As this is a practical guide, I have striven to include unwritten rules and popular conventions alongside the technical basics.

Mission and Vision

You're organizing a debate tournament, not launching a transnational corporation—Why do you need "mission and vision"?

Whatever your reservations, this double-barreled question is worth investing a little time in. They are the two questions to answer before you do anything else. First, you should define what you want to achieve. "I want to run a competition!" I hear you shout. But why? Is it to put your society on the debating map? Is it to raise money for the rest of the year? Is it to improve adjudication standards in your club? Is it to help the Convenor improve his resumé? Is it just for fun? Is it the first step toward organizing Worlds? Write down what a successful tournament means for you.

Second, you need to articulate a vision for your tournament—a written statement about what will make your tournament special. Will you have the best adjudication of any local tournament? The most free beer? The biggest prize money? The only ESL break?

You might choose to differentiate yourselves by tweaking the rules. In the UK, Cambridge has traditionally run a competition that attracts teams from all over the world, yet it is run with open motions like "This House Would Rather Be Shaken Than Stirred" —thus allowing Opening Government to choose whatever they want to debate. Nottingham has run a unique "Style IV" for several years—a kind of tournament that is in the WS family that gives greater weight to manner than does a standard tournament. While not the strictly in the Worlds Style of the World Championship, these tournaments offer choice and variety.

Think about who you want to attract and what motivates them. Also assess what is achievable given your expertise and budget. Unless you are fortunate enough to have a highly successful and respected candidate for Chief Adjudicator within your ranks, you might consider asking an outsider to come to help you.

The Organizing Committee

An organizing committee is needed to assign the tasks of preparing and running a tournament. You need a core of members who are totally committed to putting in the hard work needed to run an event. You will also need others who make smaller, yet vital, contributions on the day.

The head of an organizing committee (or OrgCom) usually holds the title of Convenor. The Convenor's job is to lead the OrgCom and take overall responsibility for the tournament. Others play important roles, but, in the final analysis, the Convenor can end up doing a lot of the work herself. The Convenor need not be a supertalented debater but should have leadership skills and commitment. The Convenor has a large number of responsibilities both before the tournament and on the day.

The elements the Convenor must consider are:

- Chief Adjudicator
- Sponsorship
- University Liaison
- Advertising
- Registration
- Venues
- Accommodations
- Food and Drink
- Social Events
- Equity
- Prizes
- Runners
- Announcements

The list is long and explains why Convenors like to have a committee of volunteers to help them. Effective delegation is essential for a large tournament and healthy for a small one. You can divide the roles and responsibilities in any number of ways to suit the strengths of your committee members and the tasks that must be accomplished. Let's go through each and show how it fits in to the typical tournament.

CHIEF ADJUDICATOR

Alongside the Convenor, the Chief Adjudicator is the most crucial person involved in running a tournament, which is why they have a section to themselves below in this chapter. The Convenor needs to find an individual with extensive adjudication experience and the ability to manage the tournament on the day. If nobody within your debate club meets that description, an outsider is usually invited to serve as Chief Adjudicator. Deputy Chief Adjudicators of upcoming global and regional championships can often be persuaded to act as Chief Adjudicators for other tournaments.

SPONSORSHIP

Debating competitions attract large numbers of intelligent, highly articulate undergraduates. Companies that recruit graduates are on the lookout for opportunities to meet the best and brightest, and some will be eager to associate their names and brands with a debating event.

If you approach companies in the right way, you may be able to attract sponsorship. If you get it wrong, you may get knocked back a few times and lose heart. Having received lots of approaches from debating societies in my days as a graduate recruiter, I must honestly say that most letters I received were terrible.

The most important rule: You must articulate the benefits that will accrue to their businesses if you hope to have them offer funds!

In general, potential sponsors will be interested in scale, prestige, and possibilities for and level of contact. The greater the number of students touched by and involved in the event, the better. The more prestigious your tournament, the more likely they are to sign on as partners. Many sponsors like to send a representative to give out material at a desk, talk to participants, and be a visible part of the grand final. This direct contact with potential employees can be valuable to them. They will also expect a mention and logo on your website, the tournament packet you hand out to participants, the program, and any similar opportunities for publicity.

Potential sponsors will be less interested in the history of your society, the rules of debate, or the item-by-item planned expenditure of your tournament. Emails that say "Can you give us $1,000? We really need it to run a tournament" should be saved for charity appeals. As a sponsor, a business expects to get something tangible for its money. Unless you keep that in mind, you are likely to be disappointed by their response.

Turn first to your natural networks. Try to find companies that have some connection with debate or with your university. Perhaps an alumnus works for them—get in touch with him or her. A former debater from your club would be ideal, but anyone who debated anywhere will understand the calibre of students likely to be involved in debate. Personal contacts tend to be more fruitful than cold calling, so do try to explore all your networks before just firing off a letter.

If you are successful in securing sponsorship and the sponsors wish to attend, you will need to appoint somebody to look after them on the day to make sure they are comfortable and that their needs are met. Also be careful to set firm boundaries. If they request a specific motion for the final or ask to adjudicate in person, think through whether you can accede to their request and still meet your objectives.

UNIVERSITY LIAISON

Some universities view their debating societies as a jewel in their crown, helping them by offering debaters extraordinary opportunities and crucial life skills. To others, debating is just another student society, standing in line for budgetary crumbs alongside the "Sub-aqua Society," "Capoeira Society," and the table tennis squad.

Whatever the debating society's standing at your institution, a closer relationship with your university leaders and decision makers can never be bad.

If you need any financial or logistical support, then the Convenor should alert university authorities in plenty of time and determine that (or if) they are supportive of your tournament. Remember, you are bringing dozens of potential students to view the campus and have an experience of the institution. If they like it, they may later decide to come to study—and pay tuition.

ADVERTISING

To make your tournament a success, you need people to attend. To get them there, they need to know it is happening. They also need to want to attend. You must advertise!

Include the following basic information in all your promotional material:

- venue
- dates and times
- team cap (the maximum number of teams you can accommodate), entrance fee per team, and the cut-off date for fee refunds
- registration deadline
- number of rounds
- the names of the core adjudication team—the Chief Adjudicator and any Deputy Chief Adjudicators

A number of websites and resources are available—make sure you take advantage of them. Here are two with the greatest audience: World Debate Website (http://flynn.debating.net) and Global Debate (globaldebateblog.blogspot.com) where you can publicize debating tournaments. As their names suggest, they have global readership and should raise awareness of your competition. You can check to ensure your date is a good one and that you haven't scheduled your event to compete with regional championships. Tournaments tend to have a Facebook group, many have a website, and any online presence *must* be regularly updated to show momentum behind your event.

If you are differentiating your tournament in some way—great socials, an amazing location, or some twist on the rules—you should highlight that information in your promotional material.

Another way of attracting attention is to make announcements and hand out flyers at other tournaments in the lead up to your own.

Finally, don't neglect the opportunity to publicize debate within your own institution. A competition is a big event and may attract new faces to come to have a look at what this debating stuff is all about. When they attend, they will see and hear great speakers in the grand final—and also fill the hall to make it a real audience event. Handled well, a tournament can be a golden opportunity to attract new club members from your own student body.

Much needs to be done; you can see a strong case for designating one person on OrgCom to take on the role of advertising your tournament.

REGISTRATION

When you advertise the tournament, be sure to include three crucial pieces of information: the team cap, the deadline for registration, and how to register.

Your team cap is the maximum number of teams you can accommodate at your tournament. The limit may be determined by the number of adjudicators you expect to have available or the number of rooms free for debates. Worlds has upward of 400 teams. The smallest viable tournaments have 16 or 20.

The deadline for registration is irrelevant if you expect to hit your team cap. But if finding teams is a struggle, it can be good to set a date and then review your progress. Let's say you budgeted for 40 teams and only 28 have registered by the week preceding your tournament. You have options—extra advertising, cutting registration fees, shaving off some costs—rather than being faced with a smaller, loss-making tournament on the day.

Registration might be done via email, your website, or telephone. The tough part is translating names on a spreadsheet into paying teams. I would strongly advise you to seek prepayment. Once teams have paid for their places, the chances of last-minute absence are reduced. But money in advance can be a struggle. You have very little leverage unless you are over-subscribed. Worlds hosts are now able to secure early payment because the competition for places is so fierce. Most tournaments have to accept fees on arrival.

Encourage teams to bring adjudicators. It may enable you to raise your team cap, giving you a larger tournament (and more registration fees). If you can, enforce the N-1 rule—this requires an institution to send a number of adjudicators equal to the number of teams minus one. Again, this will broaden the pool of adjudicators.

Everything listed above represents hard work in advance of the tournament. That's why many Organizing Committees appoint a Registration Director with responsibility for handling these issues.

When people arrive at the tournament, the work continues. You'll need a few people to write down team names, the names of individuals in each team, and the names of adjudicators—they will need a table and chairs. Teams need to pay and will want a receipt. If they need permission or passes to enter any part of the building or attend the social, you should give those out at registration. In addition, everyone will need a timetable, a map of the campus, and emergency telephone numbers in case they get lost. If you have an equity policy, attendees need to have a copy. A registration packet can be quite large.

Once registration is complete, an accurate list of teams, competitors, and adjudicators will need to be provided to the tab room.

VENUES

Debate competitions are usually held on a university campus. The finals, with the biggest audiences, are sometimes held elsewhere, often at a major landmark in the host city like a concert hall or government building. Alas, about half of the tournaments I have attended had some sort of problem with rooms.

For example, debaters show up to A14 and the room is mysteriously locked; B23 has an unscheduled Arabic class that refuses to move; C21 is open but the lights don't work. Outside the D block, workers are drilling—nobody told you in advance. The most challenging problem I ever faced was a fire alarm that developed an intermittent fault halfway through the third round. We walked up and down those stairs a lot of times.

You will need one room of a decent size (big enough to fit eight people around a table plus three judges at one end) per four teams attending. Any normal classroom will have plenty of space.

You also need a briefing room that can accommodate everybody; this room will be used to make announcements and present the draw for each round. A lecture hall or auditorium is a common solution. If you have a massive tournament, you can put speakers and adjudicators in separate halls, and either announce positions and motions simultaneously or arrange a video link from one to the other.

You also need a "tab room"—where the adjudication core can input data and handle any complaints in privacy, prizes can be stored, and the organizers can base themselves.

These are the bare minimum. You might need more. Where are people going to register when they arrive? Where will they go to hang out between rounds?

You also need to plan for contingencies. Most especially, for the situations where a room is locked, flooded, dark, or full—What is your back-up plan? Booking a couple of extra rooms in case of the unforeseen would be prudent. Debating in the quad should be a very last resort.

The most common logistical problem at debating tournaments is time overruns. If the schedule says that round three ends at 4:00, the dutiful logistics coordinator will book a room until 4:00 or 4:30. But, a tournament only progresses at the speed of the slowest adjudicator and the latest to return from lunch. Delays are not unusual, so allow a generous safety margin of two or three hours. Thus, if the round is to end at 4:00, booking the room until 6:00 or 7:00 would be safer.

ACCOMMODATIONS

The majority of university debating competitions are two-day events held over a weekend. People need somewhere to stay and will look to you for guidance.

The minimalist approach is to provide information—a list of local hotels, motels, and bed and breakfasts—leaving participants to find their own place to stay. This is cheap and easy for you, but may reduce numbers if people cannot afford to attend.

The next step up is to offer people "crash"—space on the sofas, rugs, and floors of your societies' members—with information about B&Bs, hotels, and motels for those who want to pay for extra comfort.

If you have rooms on campus, in dormitories, or are running the tournament at a hotel, then you can include accommodation in the price of the registration fee.

Be careful about prepaying for accommodation. The final number of attendees is usually lower than the number who tell you they are coming—unless you have their money in your hand. Fewer people need fewer bedrooms, so ensure that you are not left out of pocket.

Registration is the best time to hand people their keys or introduce them to their host. Make sure you keep a list of who is staying where, in case anyone gets lost, abandoned, or is late arriving back on day two.

FOOD AND DRINK

While in your care for the weekend, people will need to eat and rehydrate. Unless you are putting everyone up in expensive hotel rooms, your largest single item of expenditure is likely to be food.

If you have a cafeteria or other moderately priced food purveyors, it is reasonable to expect people to fend for themselves during rounds. But providing some kind of meal at the end of the day and breakfast in the morning is customary. Whatever you do, make sure you are open about it so that debaters know what they are getting for their registration fee.

At major tournaments, with large international contingents spending a week in a single location, food has been a thorny issue. Catering for a community including vegetarians, vegans, people with specific food allergies, as well as those requiring meat to be kosher or halal, the hosts of Worlds need to put a lot of planning into their meals. If you are providing a meal, take the time to think through these issues.

It is a common courtesy to provide water in the rooms during debates, though by no means a requirement.

SOCIAL EVENTS

In a world of rich cultural diversity, there must be an endless variety of ways that debaters like to unwind. In many places, for many people, the social is the most important part of a debating weekend. Debates come and go, and almost everyone returns home without a trophy. Yet people still come back. Time spent catching up with friends, sharing stories, and having fun is tremendously valuable to the people you want to attend.

For organizers, this involves important responsibilities. First, your social needs to be amazing. I will leave that to you. Second, give some thought to those who don't want to be part of your amazing social—Is there an alternative, somewhere else they can go? Third, you may need to think about your locality's age restrictions on consumption of alcohol.

International tournaments tend to hold social events in bars, restaurants, and nightclubs. The opportunity to drink alcohol is an expectation for many debaters. If that is not going to be a feature of your tournament, you should inform the debaters and adjudicators coming to visit you beforehand.

EQUITY

In recent years, the role of Equity Officer has emerged at major tournaments, grown in scope, and started to filter down to regional and local tournaments. The Equity Officer is responsible for ensuring that participants receive fair treatment at the tournament. He or she is designated as a person to whom debaters can complain if they believe they have been discriminated against or mistreated in any way.

In the rules, adjudicators are empowered to take action against a speaker who harasses others. An Equity Officer is for all other issues—if the harassment is by an adjudicator or outside a debate. If you decide not to appoint an Equity Officer, it is good practice to think through how you would handle such a complaint.

Happily, a very small number of complaints on grounds of equity have been made at major tournaments, and a far smaller number upheld.

PRIZES

If you ever win Worlds, you will get a trophy so large and ornate that you will struggle to get it through Customs. Expectations are much lower for other tournaments, but it is still nice to get something to commemorate your victory.

It is customary to get a cup or shield for the winning team. Beyond that, you might want to recognize, for individual prizes, the best speaker in the final (who may or may not be from the winning team) and the best speaker on the tab. Other worthy recipients might include the losing finalists, the top 10 speakers on the tab, the best novice team, and the best ESL team.

The fashion for cash prizes ebbs and flows, but if you are awarding money, normally the winning team takes the lion's share.

RUNNERS

Once the tournament begins, everything happens at breakneck speed. Communication is important to handle issues as they arise. Results need to be reported to the tab room at the earliest possible moment.

You need runners. Runners are members of your debating society wearing readily identifiable T-shirts or badges. They are there to help people when they get lost, walk competitors to their rooms, communicate to the tab room if a team doesn't show up. Runners play a critical role in ensuring a tournament runs on schedule. When the time allotted to adjudicators ends, runners take the ballot from each room and return it to the tab room. These are unglamorous tasks, but good runners are very important to any tournament. They will need to have you and your committee members express appreciation and also public recognition.

ANNOUNCEMENTS

Announcements usually are the responsibility of the Convenor who is best placed to relay information about registration, social events, accommodations, or room changes because she or he oversees these processes and ensures that they are running smoothly.

The Convenor usually welcomes everybody to the briefing room and introduces the Chief Adjudicator. Convenors keep people updated on logistics before each draw is announced and often introduce the grand final. Alongside the Chief Adjudicator, the Convenor is the public face of the tournament.

The Convenor and Chief Adjudicator have to work very closely to make a tournament run smoothly. The next section looks at the Chief Adjudicator role in detail.

Chief Adjudicator

The Chief Adjudicator (CA) is the most visible person at a debate competition. She or he delivers the briefings, handles questions, makes the major announcements, and presents the break—where the hopes and dreams of so many are confounded for another week.

Alongside the Convenor, the CA is the public face of a tournament. She also has many responsibilities behind the scenes—all to make sure the tournament runs accurately and on schedule.

At larger tournaments, the CA may also have Deputy Chief Adjudicators (DCAs) to help him with his responsibilities. Together, they are known as the core adjudication team. At Worlds, effort is made to ensure that DCAs are drawn from different parts of the globe, thus reflecting the diversity of the tournament.

The CA also may be assisted by a Tournament Director, whose grand title compensates her for the fact that her job is to run the tab. Below is a guide to the CA's responsibilities, written to aid anyone taking on this role.

TIMETABLE

The CA is responsible for the smooth running of the tournament from the moment all the teams have arrived to the presentation of prizes. Before that point, the Convenor is in command. To stop that transition in responsibility from leading to delays, the CA must be proactive in managing the timetable.

It usually works like this. Well in advance, the Convenor invites the CA, with the CA graciously accepting. The Convenor explains that a two-day competition is envisaged—with six rounds, quarter-finals, semifinals and a grand final. And a team cap of 80.

The CA gulps. There are not enough hours in the day. A time-table should be a plan, not an aspiration. The best way to design one —and I apologize if this sounds simplistic—is to fix a start point, and then add up how much time will be needed to do all you plan to do. Failure to observe this rule is the number one cause of tournaments running late.

Here is an example of a draft schedule sent to me:

Friday

6:00 PM	Registration ends
6:30	Round 1
8:00	Round 2
9:30	Social

Saturday

8:00 AM	Breakfast
9:00	Round 3
10:30	Round 4
12:00	Lunch
1:00 PM	Round 5
2:30	Round 6
4:00	Quarterfinals
5:30	Semifinals
7:00	Final
9:00	Dinner
11:00	Social

This schedule cannot work. Let's start with registration on Friday. If Registration ends promptly at 6:00, and Round 1 starts at 6:30, that leaves 30 minutes to perform the following tasks: The data must be transferred to the tab room; the teams have to be entered into the tab; the adjudicators have to be entered into the tab along with their conflicts (teams they cannot judge) and chairs nominated; if the number of teams is not a multiple of four, swing teams must be found; and a random draw must be made.

That is just about possible. But what if a team phones at 5:50 to say they are 15 minutes away? Their flight or train was delayed and they have taken a taxi to ensure they make it. Most Convenors would take a humane approach and ask the CA to delay the draw for Round 1. Should that happen—and it does, frequently—then the tournament starts late.

Now consider what must happen between 6:30 and 8:00. Swing teams must be found to cover any gaps in the draw. The draw must be presented to the teams (at 30 seconds per slide, it will take 10 minutes). The motion must be announced. Fifteen minutes must be allowed for preparation time. The debates must be held (eight speeches of seven minutes plus introductions equals an hour). The adjudicators need 10 or 15 minutes to make their decision. The results must be brought back to the tab room, entered, and checked. The draw for Round 2 must be made and adjudication panels checked for conflicts.

In the best-case scenario, I calculate that those tasks take 1 hour and 45 minutes. They could easily take two hours, if just one adjudicator starts late, a ballot paper is filled out incorrectly, or a competitor chooses the wrong moment to go to buy a sandwich.

When the second round starts and finishes late, the social is delayed, upsetting a lot of people. On day two, lunch is delayed, which means the food gets cold. Chronically late, the Convenor decides to abolish the quarterfinals and break to semis, choosing the top four teams rather than the top eight, upsetting those teams denied their expected progression. The sponsor shows up for the final on time and finds nobody there. You get the picture—and it is an unhappy, stressful picture, with lots of running and apologies.

A timetable must be realistic. Two hours between rounds is sensible for a small tournament, with a little extra time at the beginning and end of the day.

The Chief Adjudicator must help the Convenor think about the implications of the timetable for the tournament and plan accordingly.

MOTION SETTING

The Chief Adjudicator, aided by her DCAs, is responsible for setting all of the motions. Secrecy is important as debaters must not find out about a motion before it is announced. Therefore, the number of people who know the topics should be kept to an absolute minimum.

Motions should be set before the tournament. Normally, the CA wants to come up with a range of different topical issues. Breadth makes the tournament more interesting and challenging —international relations, sports, issues around reproduction, economic policy, legal reform, development, the environment, and so on. At Worlds, the core adjudication team needs to write more than 20 motions to cover the preliminaries, main break, ESL break, EFL break, and Masters, where adjudicators compete.

Motions should normally be closed. A closed motion is one that gives Opening Government a very clear idea of the policy intended. "This House Would Allow Parents Using IVF to Select the Sex of Their Child" leaves very little wiggle room for the Opening Government. They could add, "If they have already lost a child of that gender" or some other condition, though this move is hard to justify and adds as many questions as it answers. They could also, arguably, go further and say, "In fact, we have no objection to any genetic engineering of children," a bolder position. But, they could not argue that IVF should be banned or that doctors should select the gender or anything else that goes against the spirit of the motion. "This

House Would Talk to Terrorists" only needs the Prime Minister to fill in which terrorists, about what, to what end. It doesn't say All Terrorists, so Opening Government can decide under what circumstances talking might be appropriate.

Both are good closed motions because they enforce a Government burden; they force the Government to state and defend a case. If the second motion were reversed and worded "This House Would Never Talk to Terrorists," Opening Opposition would be forced to come up with some instance where they would talk to terrorists and defend it. In effect, the debate wouldn't truly start until the leader of the Opposition had spoken. This explains why debate motions can often sound very stark and challenging. Government is expected to support a bold change, whereas Opposition defends the status quo or an alternative path of change.

A closed motion that puts the burden on Government to devise a plan is the staple of Worlds Style debating tournaments. If the Prime Minister decides to change the subject and talk about something unintended ("By terrorists we mean peaceful environmental protesters—we should talk to them"), then adjudicators are empowered to penalize that team. If they refuse to come up with a plan and only argue that, in principle, talking to terrorists is a good idea, but not in any specific situation, then adjudicators should punish them for failure to fulfill their role.

In contrast to closed motions, open motions give almost endless leeway to teams to come up with any policy they like. Cambridge periodically used James Bond films as the theme for its tournament motions ("This House Would Sooner Be Shaken Than Stirred") and just a few seconds linking the words *shaken* and *stirred* to your favorite idea for changing the world enables you to meet this challenge.

Open motions have become less fashionable as tournaments try to attract speakers preparing for Worlds by offering an experience as close as possible to the genuine article, with no variations at all. I think this is unfortunate. Open motions are the best possible training for Opening Opposition, who have no idea what case to oppose until the Prime Minister opens his mouth. If you can cope with that, you can cope with anything. Closing Government also benefits from the added challenges of creating new arguments in favor of an unfamiliar proposition, without the benefit of preparation time.

Analysis debates are a more recent innovation. When a Chief Adjudicator sets an analysis debate, he or she announces the fact to debaters, signaling that they should treat it differently. Rather than coming up with a definition that proposes taking action, in these debates, Opening Government is expected to argue that the motion is true. The other teams are also supposed to address this question of truth.

Examples of analysis debate motions are:

- This House Believes Iraq Is Better Off Now Than Before the War
- This House Believes Feminism Has Damaged Motherhood
- This House Believes the Welfare State Has Hurt the Poor

Analysis debates are rare, but as they occasionally happen at Worlds and regional tournaments, they are sometimes set at university competitions to help debaters practice for them.

If you need inspiration to generate motions, websites containing thousands of ideas and examples from the past are available with the click of a mouse. But the best motions are current and live— not theoretical constructs but issues that affect people's lives today. Even if they are twists on old topics, you can do worse than opening the week's newspapers and picking out stories. Having a team of DCAs certainly helps to spread the load.

The topics for the European Universities' Debating Championships in Tallinn, Estonia, at which I was Chief Adjudicator, were:

ROUND 1: This House Would Require People to Work in Return for Welfare Payments

ROUND 2: This House Believes That Sporting Bodies Should Penalize Teams When Their Players Commit Criminal Acts Off the Field

ROUND 3: This House Would Use Military Force Where Necessary to Deliver Emergency Aid

ROUND 4: This House Would Make Fines Relative to Wealth

ROUND 5: This House Would Ban the Physical Punishment of Children by Parents

ROUND 6: This House Believes Developed Countries Should Not Accept Skilled Migrants from Developing Countries

ROUND 7: This House Would Pay Morbidly Obese People to Lose Weight

QUARTERFINALS: This House Would Ban the Broadcast of Recordings Produced by Terrorists

ESL QUARTERFINALS: This House Would Require All Schools to Teach Safe Sex to Children from Age 10 Regardless of Parental Consent

SEMIFINALS: This House Would Abolish Income Tax

ESL SEMIFINALS: This House Believes the European Union Should Declare That Energy Security Is a Legitimate Reason for Military Action

FINAL: This House Would Ban Nazi and Soviet Symbols

ESL FINAL: This House Would Allow Soldiers to Opt Out of Individual Conflicts for Personal Reasons

A team of five people needed several hours to come up with a long list, cut it down to a short list, and adjust the wording until we could find a form with which we were all satisfied. Note how these motions all require Government to propose a course of action.

BRIEFING

Every tournament starts with a briefing by the Chief Adjudicator. He will introduce himself and the DCAs, then together they will provide participants with all the information they need to understand and take part in the tournament.

Speakers need to know how many rounds to expect, the length of speeches, and after which rounds they can expect verbal feedback. Adjudicators need to understand their duties. How long do they have to make a decision? What happens to their ballot? They also need to know when verbal adjudication ends. Most tournaments do not reveal results in the last one or two preliminary rounds to keep an element of suspense surrounding the break.

At major tournaments, briefing can be a long process. Sometimes, organizers offer an optional separate briefing that reviews the rules for beginners. A main briefing is always held; its purpose is to recap the rules and detail the core adjudication team's interpretation of key points in the rules. They may have specific areas that they want to highlight and encourage.

Debaters usually ask plenty of questions at a briefing. The CA must make sure the chief adjudication pool has agreed on an answer before committing to a position. Getting back to someone after conferring with the team is better than tying yourself to a mistake.

Last, perhaps most important, the CA should try to make the briefing fun and welcoming. She has anything from 10 minutes to an hour of people's attention. The CA is the only person standing between debaters and their judges and the competition. It is a chance to set a great tone for the weekend.

ADJUDICATOR ASSIGNMENT

At major tournaments, great care is taken to ensure the fairness of rankings for adjudicators. There are potentially more than 300 adjudicators, with varying levels of skills and experience, and just a handful of people in the adjudication core who have little to no knowledge about most of them.

To enable the CA to rank adjudicators, they are often asked to do two things. The first is to submit a CV detailing their speaking and adjudication achievements to date. If you judged the final of your home tournament, this is the place to write it down. Speaking achievements are not weighted as highly as adjudication experience —they are two different sets of skills—but are taken as indicative of the level of debate with which someone is comfortable.

The CA may ask potential adjudicators to take an adjudication test. Organizers can either play a recorded debate or arrange for a live debate. The risk of a recorded debate is that one or more of the adjudicators may have seen it before and won't come to it with a fresh mind or may know the result. One risk of a live debate is that it is horribly one-sided and does not give any scope for differentiation, as practically everyone has the same result. The much greater risk is that your live debate will be messy, close, difficult to disentangle, and, while your adjudicators come up with different decisions, so does the core adjudication team. A test needs a standard by which people's responses can be measured; if significant disagreement arises among the CA and DCAs about the result, it can hamper your efforts to rank people. Given these risks, I recommend a staged debate between well-matched teams, recorded behind closed doors, and marked in advance by the Chief Adjudication team. If that is too much work, have a live debate and keep your fingers crossed!

Drawing on the CVs and the test results, the CA and DCAs give every adjudicator an initial ranking between 50 and 100; following registration, this ranking is entered into the tab. When round one is drawn, those with the highest rankings will chair rooms and the rest will be wings. This ranking can be reviewed throughout the tournament based on feedback. This whole process is data-driven, which gives a sense of process and fairness to decisions.

It is widely accepted, at smaller tournaments, that the CA will need to use her discretion to establish who should chair and who should wing, without going through these formal processes. If you don't know many people, you can ask for CVs and use them as a basis. Otherwise, consult your DCAs or speak informally to those with greater knowledge of the individuals in question.

Results and the Speaker Scale

The CA is ultimately responsible for ensuring the right results are entered into the tab, though the Tournament Director is usually the person who manually enters them. Accordingly, the CA needs to insist that a strict process be followed to get ballots to the rooms and accurate results from the rooms.

RESULTS

Accurate results rely on a robust process being followed across the tournament. Every Chair should take a ballot from the briefing room to his room. Depending on the tab program in use, this ballot may already have the room number, teams, speakers, and team positions nicely printed out.

If not, or if anything is missing, the Chair is still responsible for making sure that results are filled in properly. Before the debate begins, the Chair should check the team names and ask the order of speakers for each team. When the debate is over and the panel discussion has come to a close, he should take responsibility for filling in the final decision on the ballot.

Mistakes can happen. The most common mistake to avoid is confusing team points (3, 2, 1, 0) with position (1st, 2nd, 3rd, 4th), so a well-designed ballot asks the Chair to write in both next to each team. The second most common mistake is getting aggregate speaker points wrong. The third, and hardest to detect, is confusing the two speakers within a team and swapping their speaker points.

Results should be returned to the tab room before verbal adjudication begins. If runners are available, the Chair should fold the ballot and give it to them. If not, a wing judge should be sent to the tab room. Although the result is open, the speaker points are still confidential until the end of the tournament.

SPEAKER SCALE

When I started debating, three separate speaker scales were in common use: the 30-point scale, 40-point scale, and 100-point scale. Not only was there no standardization between scales—within those competitions that preferred the 30-point scale, some used the whole scale, whereas others started at 15 and went no higher than 26. Each adjudicator had her own idea, or no idea, about how to assign points to speakers. Now the 100-point scale is ubiquitous and adjudicators are much clearer about the meaning of a 55, 70, or 85. Below is the standard from the Worlds rules:

GRADE	MARK	MEANING
A	90–100	Excellent to flawless. The standard of speech you would expect to see from a speaker at the semifinal/grand final level of the tournament. This speaker has many strengths and few, if any, weaknesses.
B	80–89	Above-average to very good. The standard you would expect to see from a speaker at the finals level or in contention to make the finals. This speaker has clear strengths and some minor weaknesses.
C	70–79	Average. The speaker has strengths and weaknesses in roughly equal proportions.
D	60–69	Poor to below-average. The speaker has clear problems and some minor strengths.
E	50–59	Very poor. This speaker has fundamental weaknesses and few, if any, strengths.

What is crucial to make the standard work is that adjudicators apply it universally. A speech should not receive a 90 simply because it is a speech in the final at Worlds. Sometimes a Worlds final is not a great debate. A speech deserving a 90 or above is a speech of the very highest quality, one of the best eight speakers in the world in top form. It is no good treating a 90 as the level of speech you would expect to see in the final of your local tournament. A 90 should be a 90 wherever the speech is made, not relative to the level of any given tournament. It takes experience to make those judgments, which is why the most experienced Chair is put in charge of leading the process of assigning speaker marks.

Remember, also, that speaker points are secondary to team points. The aggregate speaker points of each team must correspond to their position in the debate.

Any ballot that is filled out incorrectly must be returned to the Chair of that room, who must correct it to ensure that the team judged to be first has the most points, the team coming in last the least, and those in between the right distribution. Making a mistake on speaker points holds up the tournament and causes general consternation in the tab room. The Chair should double-check the ballot before returning it.

Tabulation

The tab is a system for recording results and determining who debates against whom. It is normally controlled by one person—a separate Tournament Director or the Chief Adjudicator. The subject of tabulation could take an entire book, although I doubt anyone would read it. I will be brief and concentrate on the essentials.

Long gone are the days when finalists were selected by the CA wandering around, having chats with a few trusted lieutenants, asking, "Have you seen anyone really good?" Gone also are the days when a team was assigned Opening Government seven times out of nine in their preliminary rounds at Worlds. Debating in all the positions is standard for a modern tab. The times when systems packed up altogether and whole rounds had to be cut are also receding into distant memory.

The rules and conventions about how to tabulate are important to master if you are putting on a tournament. Doing things your own way might seem trivial and convenient to you, but you are likely to upset a lot of people—who perceive the tried-and-tested way as the fairest.

To assist, here's an example of the basic principles behind tabulation of a tournament.

Round 1 should be assigned randomly. It doesn't matter if Nabanda's four teams flew 6,000 miles to your tournament and yet end up debating one another—there is no cause to alter the draw for any reason. From Round 2 onward, teams should be "power-paired," competing against teams that have achieved the same level of success so far.

Step 1 is to create a table of teams in order of team points. Those teams that have the same number of team points are then ranked by speaker points, as follows:

TEAM NAME	TEAM POINTS	SPEAKER POINTS	POSITION
Steel A	3	165	1
Caxford B	3	154	2
MST A	2	161	3
MST B	2	152	4
Lardon	1	155	5
Abifield	1	151	6
Steel B	0	140	7
Caxford A	0	136	8

Step 2 is to put together the teams with the highest number of team points—in this case, neatly, Steel A, Caxford B, MST A, and MST B will debate together, leaving Lardon, Abifield, Steel B, and Caxford A in the other room.

Step 3 is to impose the respective team positions that maximize each team's opportunity to debate each of the four positions an equal number of times across the tournament. So, if Steel A has already been Closing Opposition, they should not be Closing Opposition again in Round 2.

Let's look again at the tab after Round 2. Step 1 remains the same: Create a table of teams in order of team points and speaker points.

TEAM NAME	TEAM POINTS	SPEAKER POINTS	POSITION
Steel A	6	321	1
MST A	4	315	2
Abifield	3	305	3
Caxford B	3	304	4
Caxford A	3	296	5
MST B	3	288	6
Lardon	2	292	7
Steel B	0	264	8

Our Step 2 is more complicated this time. Abifield, Caxford B, Caxford A, and MST B all have the same number of team points. In this situation, the tab program should select, at random, two of these four teams to take on Steel A and MST A in Round 3. The purpose is to avoid rewarding a team for achieving lower speaker points by placing them in rooms with weaker teams.

You then repeat this process through all of the rounds until the break. It is the simplest policy, and it is how Worlds and other major tournaments are run. However, if you are running a small tournament, you might want to experiment with something slightly different for the last preliminary round: folding.

Folding is a procedure that aims to protect teams who have debated well throughout a tournament from the likelihood of dropping out in the final round. Let's say you have 32 teams and you are breaking to semifinals. It is entirely plausible that the teams ranked 1–4 and those ranked 5–8 will face each other in the last preliminary round. Because somebody has to come in third and fourth in every debate, four of those top eight teams might very well not progress, having been beaten by the best in the final preliminary round. You might just say, "Well, to win a tournament, you have to beat the best." Or, you might protect those teams who have done well consistently by folding the top 16 teams. The choice is yours.

Folding means assigning the teams in the following positions together:

1, 8, 9, 16
2, 7, 10, 15
3, 6, 11, 14
4, 5, 12, 13

On paper, the top teams have an easier route to the semifinals. They have been seeded, thus are facing teams that have been less successful up to that point. But if, for example, the sixteenth-ranked team does manage to win their final round, they may yet make the break.

If you follow steps 1–3 for each round, remember to keep a separate speaker tab where a debater's individual marks are recorded, and carry out your decision about whether to fold the last preliminary round, you have mastered all the essentials of tabbing.

You can either fiddle around in Excel creating your own formulas to achieve this, or—and here is some very good news—resources are available to help you. The best one I have worked with is Tabbie, a simple-to-use and reliable open source software found at http://tabbie.wikidot.com/start. It was developed for Worlds in Singapore in 2004, where I was a DCA, and has been improved by several people since.

A great advantage of Tabbie is that it allows you to be precise about where you assign adjudicators. You can enter and update a rating for each judge, then, at any time, you can change the formula by which you assign them. Thus, you can have all your strongest adjudicators as Chairs early in the tournament, then, when it becomes numerically impossible for some teams to break later on, put two experienced judges in your top rooms to ensure that the best possible decisions are made where it counts.

Once the preliminary rounds are over, your tabbing work is almost done. Competitors will expect a printout of the team tab (showing the final rankings) and the speaker tab to compare notes, curse their bad luck, and see where they went right or wrong.

Feedback on Adjudicators

Feedback on adjudicators is really useful to the core adjudication team. Your initial ranking of judges can always be improved based on observations made during the tournament. This can either be formalized, as it is at major tournaments, or kept to informal conversations; either way, you should remain open to adjudicators moving up and down your ranking.

A formal system involves a lot of paper. Teams are each given a feedback form on which they write whether they came 1st, 2nd, 3rd, or 4th and how satisfied they were with the Chair's verbal adjudication. This helps to assess how the various Chairs are doing. Treat this kind of feedback with caution. If the teams who came 1st, 2nd, and 3rd all gave great feedback to the Chair, but the last-place team said she was terrible, that colors the reliability of that feedback. However, if a winning team complain that the decision was a poor one, you know you have a situation worth investigating.

In addition to these forms, all of which must be read and considered by the CA and DCAs, there are forms for the Chair in each room to give feedback on their wings. The purpose of these is to identify potential Chairs, perhaps less experienced adjudicators who have quickly found their feet, and to spot those who can't or won't apply the rules.

If your tournament is smaller, you might choose to keep these chats informal. It is a good idea to hear from Chairs about wings with potential. Teams should be free to come to you if they feel a decision was not justified by the rules. You can't change the results! But you can assign one of your team to judge with someone whose adjudication has come into question and then form your own opinion.

Whatever the process, if you are using Tabbie, you can record changes by altering the number assigned to each adjudicator up or down. Otherwise, you will need to keep notes and check your panels manually.

Handling Complaints

Complaints are part of any competitive activity. Debate is no different. Should debaters or other adjudicators feel that something inappropriate has taken place in a debate, the Chief Adjudicator has the ultimate responsibility of ensuring that the issue is resolved.

Nobody, not even the Chief Adjudicator, can change the result of a debate once a decision has been made. Whatever result comes back on the ballot from a Chair is always entered into the tab. Within each debate, the adjudicators in the room decide the placings and speaker points. However eloquently you recount the tale, the CA has no power to alter the decisions made by those who saw the debate.

If adjudicators feel that a speaker has harassed another person, then they may give them zero speaker points. This is a decision without appeal and extremely infrequent. The matter will not normally end there. Unacceptable behavior may lead to additional action from the organizers or even the host university if it has a harassment policy that a debater is alleged to have breached.

If the adjudicators do not act, and a debater feels that the behavior of another speaker was unacceptable, this is a matter for the Equity Officer (if you appoint one) or the Convenor to handle. Should a debater feel that an adjudicator behaved inappropriately, then the hearing should involve both the Chief Adjudicator and the Equity Officer (if you appoint one) or the Convenor. Unless a formal process has been put in place, the usual approach is to first hear the complaint, then the adjudicator's side of the story, call witnesses if necessary, and then take action. An adjudicator could be kicked out or, depending on the findings, no action might be taken.

Ninety-nine percent of complaints are about the result. Of those, most are made by teams finishing third and fourth, who felt that they should have come in first or second. Complaints can be minimized if a formal process exists for handling feedback on Chairs.

The CA will only take action, under normal circumstances, if there is a pattern of bad feedback on a certain adjudicator. Comments from a winning team that criticize the Chair will carry special weight, because, presumably, there is no self-interest behind them. Possible action includes "babysitting"—putting an experienced judge with the adjudicator in question for a round to check out how he performs—or downgrading him from a Chair to a Wing for future rounds.

The Break

Most teams go out at the break, so it is a moment of emotion. It can also be a moment of drama, particularly at Worlds with hundreds of people drowning out the sound system, yet listening intently for their team name to be called.

The convention is for the CA to announce the break rather than displaying it on a big screen. The successful teams are called in first-to-last order: "Breaking first, with 10 points, Abifield A" and so on. Speak clearly! Mumbling has led many a team to celebrate too soon.

Often the pool of adjudicators required for knockout rounds is also announced and recognized. It is a great opportunity to thank all those helpers, runners, adjudicators, and teams whose services are no longer required.

ESL

If you are running a separate ESL break, you need to plan in advance.

First, be clear about your eligibility criteria. You could operate a system based on trust, which accepts that anyone who shows up and claims to speak English as a second language can compete as ESL. Alternatively (as is done at major tournaments), you might try to police it, setting criteria and interviewing individuals to check that they qualify.

Second, decide whether you want to recognize individual speakers or just teams. If you don't have a top ESL speaker award but do plan an ESL final, then this decision will be easy! Whatever you decide, the information needs to be fixed and finalized before the tournament begins because it has to be entered into the tab.

Third, think through your policy if an ESL-eligible team or teams make it to the main break as well as the ESL break. Will you allow them to compete in both? Will you only permit them to speak in the main break, allowing another team the opportunity to compete in the ESL break? Competitors deserve to know the ground rules in advance.

When it comes to the break, make sure to retain enough adjudicators to cover the ESL break rounds as well. Think about whether you want to assign your best adjudicators to the ESL final, as if it had equal status to the grand final, or use it as opportunity to bring in other judges.

Be careful about the way you treat the ESL break. It can cause unintended offense if people make announcements about the English as a First Language break—there is no such thing!—it is the main break, open to all. If you schedule the ESL final at the same time as the main break semifinals, it similarly suggests that you don't believe an ESL team could make those semis. Given that you are going to the trouble of recognizing excellence among ESL speakers, it would be perverse if you ended up upsetting them through carelessness.

Elimination Rounds

Elimination rounds have a particular pattern of seeding to reward teams who have been most successful in the preliminary rounds.

There is a convention governing how teams break. It should follow the pattern of folding I set forth earlier: [1, 8, 9, 16], [2, 7, 10, 15], [3, 6, 11, 14], [4, 5, 12, 13] if 16 teams break; [1, 4, 5, 8] and [2, 3, 6, 7] if 8 teams break.

If you have quarterfinals, then when you move to semis, you should fold the teams again: The two teams progressing from [1, 8, 9, 16] should compete against the two teams who make it through [4, 5, 12, 13] while the two teams progressing from [2, 7, 10, 15] meet two from [3, 6, 11, 14]. It is possible, using this system, that two teams, if they keep progressing, will meet each other in the quarterfinals, semifinals, and final!

In elimination rounds, the adjudication panel is often expanded from three to five, seven, or nine. Until the final, their job is to advance two teams. No winner is announced, no order, no speaker points, no verbal feedback. With larger panels, reaching agreement (and thus the result) can take a long time. The CA's job is to impose discipline and keep things moving.

After the cameral feel of preliminary rounds, elimination rounds can generate a bit of audience participation. If one team from an institution breaks, often the others will stay to cheer them on. In international tournaments, patriotism can stir people to support other universities. It all adds to the excitement.

The Final

At a final, plenty is usually going on besides debating. Representatives of the sponsors, the university hierarchy, students from the host university, even members of the public may come to get an experience of debate by attending your final. They need to be welcomed and warmed up—this is traditionally part of the Convenor's role. The motion is announced and teams are given the usual 15 minutes to prepare while a series of announcements, reflections, and thanks are offered.

The final will have a panel of seven or nine adjudicators. A Speaker, facing the audience, is appointed to keep order, introduce the debaters, and keep time. When the adjudicators retire to deliberate, the wait begins for a decision. Typically, at least 20 minutes pass before a final panel reaches a decision—it can take as long as 2 hours, unless the CA is firm about bringing the matter to a vote. As the CA chairs the final panel, it is within his or her power.

Some tournaments fill this wait with a floor debate. Anyone from the audience can come forward and make a short speech in furtherance of the Government or Opposition. By alternating between the two sides, the Speaker can ensure the debate continues even after the final has concluded. It is a great way to keep people involved and, if your invited sponsor/faculty/public want a result to round off their evening, a good time filler. But floor debates have been mocked as a chance for those who didn't make the final to show why.

The alternative path, more often taken, is to leave the adjudicators sweating and fighting in a small room while everyone else goes to the dinner or social event. However long the panel takes to confer, people are enjoying themselves—except for those teams sweating on the results! Once the decision is in, the CA will announce it. Prizes are usually given for best speaker, top speaker on the tab, and so on, before the winning team is finally declared.

The debating is over and the fun can begin.

Conclusion

My book ends where it began—your debate club. I have given you advice covering rules, roles, definitions, cases, clash, arguments, rebuttal, style, structure, and adjudication. I have tried to help you enter and hold competitions, so you can get the most out of them. I have endeavored to stay practical, equipping you to cope in any situation a debate might throw at you.

But the only place you can truly learn to debate is in a debate. A thriving debate club, holding internal training, offering adjudication experience, sending you to competitions, running an annual tournament, gives you a place to try out new techniques and embed skills.

To conclude, I would like to suggest ways you can take your debate club meetings to the next level.

Variety

Rather than just having a debate every week, try to mix things up. A full Worlds Style debate, plus time for preparation and adjudication, can take a full two hours, so it can be hard to find additional time for skill development outside a single debate. Hold training sessions in some weeks that focus on particular skills. This book, and feedback at competitions, can help you identify areas for improvement. Don't be afraid to repeat fun exercises and simple drills. Involve your most experienced speakers to improve mental dexterity and get people talking. Great sportsmen practice the basics every day, so don't feel that any of these activities are too simple to warrant your time.

When you do hold debates, once people are used to Worlds Style, start experimenting with the format. Set an open motion to really challenge those in Opening Opposition and Closing Government. Judge solely or predominantly on manner one week. Try two-against-two debates, with just Opening Government and Opening Opposition, to practice case development in the top half of a debate. Shorten speeches to five minutes and see how it affects structure. You can do so much to play with the parameters of a debate and test people's ability to adapt.

Expertise

Use every last bit of knowledge and skill at your disposal. When you send people to tournaments, as speakers or adjudicators, get them to share what they learned with the whole club. Make them prepare a short session on their top tip. Experience needs to be recycled.

Utilize all the resources you can get your hands on to train debaters properly. Books, online tutorials, video recordings of debates are all at your disposal. Giving uninformed feedback can set back a group of novice debaters despite the best intentions of the coach. Worlds Style debate is what it is, not what you or I want it to be. We have a duty to teach debaters how to succeed and to be clear where we deviate from that approach to let speakers make up their own minds.

Invite trainers to visit your debate club and teach you. The worst they can say is "no." For the cost of travel and an overnight sofa, you may well be able to attract an experienced debater to come to visit you. The debating circuit has a great tradition of passing on knowledge and expertise.

Opportunity

Give people incentives to be a part of your club. Send as many as possible to competitions. Make your sessions inclusive and your training relevant to newcomers. Avoid jargon and keep things informal.

Invite other clubs to come and experience what you are doing—internally and externally. Undoubtedly, some students at your institution are interested in the issues you discuss but don't attend your meetings. Get them there—just once—and there's a good chance they will come again.

Find forums and opportunities for debate. Keep up-to-date not only with tournaments and conferences but also with online competitions that can help to develop critical skills—for example, the World Online Debating Championships (http://debatewise.org/wodc).

Whatever you do, wherever debating takes you—enjoy it and good luck.

APPENDIXES

A

Online Resources

Here is a list of popular online resources used by debaters to help improve their skills and find out what is happening in the world of competitive debate.

WORLD DEBATE WEBSITE
http://flynn.debating.net

The World Debate Website was built and is maintained by Colm Flynn, assisted by a network of content editors across the world. It is the hub for information about Worlds Style tournaments. Colm is a former Chair of Worlds Council and Deputy Chief Adjudicator of Worlds and knows as much about debating as anyone on the planet. His site is a remarkable compendium of information, history, and help. You can find advice on how to debate, opinions on adjudication, links to tab programs, lists of motions, and results going back to the late nineties. It is the first place you should go to find out what's happening in the world of debate.

GLOBAL DEBATE BLOG
http://globaldebateblog.blogspot.com

Alfred Snider is an inspired and tireless advocate of debate. He is the Lawrence Professor of Forensics at the University of Vermont and has almost forty years' experience in debating. A strong advocate of Worlds Style, he does more and goes further than anyone else to bring debate opportunities to those who need the skills. His site contains news of upcoming events, articles, and information relevant to those interested in debate and world events. It is a must read.

INTERNATIONAL DEBATE EDUCATION ASSOCIATION
http://www.idebate.org

The IDEA website is full of useful resources to improve debating skills, though its scope goes way beyond Worlds Style to other types of debate and uses of the spoken word. Debatepedia is designed to become the Wikipedia of debate; Debatabase contains pros and cons for more than five hundred topics. There are also plenty of videos to explore.

DEBATEWISE
http://www.debatewise.org

The home of online debate, Debatewise features arguments on a wide range of current topics and boasts a searchable resource of all its debates going back over several years. It is a great place to hone your analytical skills, comment on others' arguments, vote on debates, and enter a community of online debaters. Debatewise also hosts the annual World Online Debating Championships.

BRITISH DEBATE
http://www.britishdebate.com/calendar

Despite its name, the British Debate calendar carries listings of tournaments held across Europe. If you are based in Europe or coming to Europe and want to know what opportunities are available, BD (as it is fondly known) will tell you what tournaments are coming up.

Definitional Challenges

Whenever I give a briefing at a major tournament, I get asked a question about definitional challenges.

Yet as a judge, I have only seen a definitional challenge in perhaps 1 percent of debates.

People are fascinated by the worst case scenario and desperate to know what to do. "If Opening Government squirrels [set a definition outside the spirit of the motion] and Opening Opposition gives a bad definition, then Opening Government doesn't accept their definition, then Closing Government comes up with another definition, do we in Closing Opposition follow Opening Government, Closing Government, or our colleagues in Opening Opposition?" It is bizarre what keeps people awake at night.

The really useful advice—"Just debate better than them"— doesn't get to the heart of the technical question, so is unsatisfactory to the questioner. Let's take a look at the rules in detail:

The definition must:

(a) have a clear and logical link to the motion—an average reasonable person would accept the link made by the member between the motion and the definition (where there is no such link, the definition is sometimes referred to as a "squirrel");

(b) not be self-proving—a definition is self-proving when the case is that something should or should not be done and there is no reasonable rebuttal. A definition may also be self-proving when the case is that a certain state of affairs exists or does not exist and there is no reasonable rebuttal (these definitions are sometimes referred to as "truisms");

(c) not be time set—the debate must take place in the present and the definition cannot set the debate in the past or the future; and

(d) not be place set unfairly—the definition cannot restrict the debate so narrowly to a particular geographical or political location that a participant of the tournament could not reasonably be expected to have knowledge of the place.

Let's take the motion "This House Would Ban Euthanasia" and play around with some dodgy definitions.

If Opening Government defines as "we will ban assisted suicide," it may be argued that they have moved away from the intended subject matter as euthanasia involves the mortal act being made by somebody else, usually a doctor. But the average reasonable person is not supposed to be a pedant. A challenge of this definition under (a) would be ludicrous.

Compare this definition. "Euthanasia means 'good death' in Greek; and the 'good death' of the Greek economy was the 2010 bailout by Germany; so we would ban all bailouts of Eurozone economies." That is a squirrel and could be challenged under (a).

"Euthanasia was practiced by the Nazis. It is the killing of people, by doctors, without their consent. It should be banned." This definition falls under (b). It is implicit in the motion that we are talking about voluntary euthanasia. There is no reasonable rebuttal to the contention that people should not be murdered by doctors. Opposition cannot be compelled to make that case.

"By 2030, at the current rate of development, advancements in palliative care will be such that no one will ever have to live in pain. When that happens, euthanasia should be banned." This innovative thought experiment falls foul of (c) as it is set in the future.

Most Opening Governments would not bother setting the motion "This House Would Ban Euthanasia" in one country, preferring instead to say that all countries should pursue their policy. Others might choose to put it in a major/well-known country that has legalized euthanasia, while giving some information about the background there. These options would not give rise to a successful challenge. But consider the following: "We believe that voluntary euthanasia should be banned in San Marino. Now on to our arguments. First, life is sacred . . ."

San Marino is one of the world's oldest sovereign states, a landlocked 24 square miles surrounded by Italy, and is a member of the United Nations. Its population is 97 percent Catholic and might be presumed to take a view convenient to the Government's case. But only 31,000 people live in San Marino. There is no good reason to center your case there. It is unfair to expect a participant at a tournament to have knowledge of that country.

Tactically, I would still advise debaters not to challenge this definition. You can point out that Opening Government is running scared, then use general arguments to show that euthanasia should be legal everywhere, including San Marino. But the rules afford you the opportunity to challenge.

I hope you can see how outlandish a definition must be to warrant a challenge. But if you need to make one, let's see how the rules tell you to do it:

Challenging the Definition

The Leader of the Opposition may challenge the definition if it violates the rules above. She should clearly state that she is challenging the Prime Minister's definition and then offer an alternative.

There is all the difference in the world between a whinge and a challenge. A whinge is when the Leader of the Opposition gets up and complains: "I wasn't expecting to talk about assisted suicide, I don't understand why we're talking about San Marino, and I think Opening Government is clueless about this topic" before going on to make the case they thought up during prep time.

This is not a definitional challenge. Many times, debaters have come up to me and said, "But I challenged the definition!" when they didn't. Complaining about the definition is not the same as challenging it.

You need to say the magic words "I challenge this definition" and follow it up with your own—in this instance, given you are on Opposition—"We think everyone should have legal access to voluntary euthanasia."

So, we have a challenge. How will the adjudicators respond?

Assessing the Definitional Challenge

The adjudicators should determine the definition to be "unreasonable" where it violates the rules above. The onus to establish that the definition is unreasonable is not on the adjudicators, however, but on the members asserting that the definition is unreasonable—they must provide a reasonable alternative.

Here's the catch: The adjudicators don't and mustn't tell you what they are thinking. So, all eyes focus on the Deputy Prime Minister, who, in turn, will be scanning the adjudication panel for visual clues of their view on the reasonableness of the definition. He has to decide whether to turn on his partner (and come a near-certain fourth) or stick with him and leave his fate to the judges. Unsurprisingly, the top half of a debate with a challenge typically features four people talking at cross-purposes.

Now for the worst case scenario in the rules:

> Where the definition of the Opening Government is unreasonable and an alternative definition is substituted by the Opening Opposition, the Closing Government may introduce matter which is inconsistent with the matter presented by the Opening Government and consistent with the definition of the Opening Opposition.
>
> If the Opening Opposition has substituted a definition that is also unreasonable, the Closing Government may challenge the definition of the Opening Opposition and substitute an alternative definition.
>
> If the Closing Government has substituted a definition that is also unreasonable (in addition to the unreasonable definitions of the Opening Government and Opening Opposition), the Closing Opposition may challenge the definition of the Closing Government and substitute an alternative definition.

The Member for the Government has a choice: Accept that Opening Opposition's definition is reasonable and go with it, jettisoning Opening Government, or redefine. Here, a second choice emerges: support the original definition by Opening Government or create an all-new definition for the second half of the debate.

As Member for the Opposition, if you are still thinking about definitions by the time the debate reaches you, something has gone horribly wrong and your thoughts should turn to other, life-enriching hobbies to which your precious weekends might be devoted. Nevertheless, you might take a moment to consider your options. You can accept Closing Government's definition if it is reasonable. If it isn't, you can redefine, accepting Opening Opposition's definition or suggesting your own. The only option not open to you, unless Closing Government supported Opening Government's definition, is to take the dramatically satisfying path of going back to the beginning and arguing against Opening Government's definition.

I have only witnessed the worst case scenario once, and that was more than ten years ago. There is no skill less worth your time and worry than how to challenge.

C

WUDC World Parliamentary Debating Rules

Part 1—Introduction

1.1   The format of the debate

1.1.1   The debate will consist of four teams of two persons (persons will be known as "members"), a chairperson (known as the "Speaker of the House" or "Mister/Madame Speaker" and a panel of adjudicators. In the absence of a chairperson, the Chair of the panel of adjudicators will act as the chairperson.

1.1.2   Teams will consist of the following members:

Opening Government:
"Prime Minister" or "First Government member" and
"Deputy Prime Minister" or "Second Government member";

Opening Opposition:
"Leader of the Opposition" or "First Opposition member" and

N.B. The numbering, order and wording of these rules reflects a proposed tidy-up put to Worlds Council 2012.

"Deputy Leader of the Opposition" or "Second Opposition member";

Closing Government:

"Member for the Government" or "Third Government member" and

"Government Whip" or "Fourth Opposition member";

Closing Opposition:

"Member for the Opposition" or "Third Opposition member" and

"Opposition Whip" or "Fourth Opposition member."

1.1.3 Members will deliver substantive speeches in the following order:

(1) Prime Minister;

(2) Opposition Leader;

(3) Deputy Prime Minister;

(4) Deputy Opposition Leader;

(5) Member for the Government;

(6) Member for the Opposition;

(7) Government Whip;

(8) Opposition Whip.

1.1.4 Members will deliver a substantive speech of seven minutes duration and should offer Points of Information while members of the opposing teams are speaking.

1.2 The motion

1.2.1 The motion should be unambiguously worded.

1.2.2 The motion should reflect that the World Universities Debating Championship is an international tournament.

1.2.3 The members should debate the motion in the spirit of the motion and the tournament.

1.3   Preparation

1.3.1   The debate should commence 15 minutes after the motion is announced.

1.3.2   Teams should arrive at their debate within five minutes of the scheduled starting time for that debate.

1.3.3   Members are permitted to use printed or written material during preparation and during the debate. Printed material includes books, journals, newspapers and other similar materials. The use of electronic equipment is prohibited during preparation and in the debate.

1.4   Points of Information

1.4.1   Points of Information (questions directed to the member speaking) may be asked between first minute mark and the six-minute mark of the members' speeches (speeches are of seven minutes duration).

1.4.2   To ask a Point of Information, a member should stand, place one hand on his or her head and extend the other towards the member speaking. The member may announce that they would like to ask a "Point of Information" or use other words to this effect.

1.4.3   The member who is speaking may accept or decline to answer the Point of Information.

1.4.4   Points of Information should not exceed 15 seconds in length.

1.4.5   The member who is speaking may ask the person offering the Point of Information to sit down where the offeror has had a reasonable opportunity to be heard and understood.

1.4.6   Members should attempt to answer at least two Points of Information during their speech. Members should also offer Points of Information.

1.4.7   Points of Information should be assessed in accordance with clause 4.3.4 of these rules.

1.4.8 Points of Order and Points of Personal Privilege are not permitted.

1.5 Timing of the speeches

1.5.1 Speeches should be seven minutes in duration (this should be signalled by two strikes of the gavel). Speeches over seven minutes and 15 seconds may be penalized.

1.5.2 Points of Information may only be offered between the first minute mark and the six minute mark of the speech (this period should be signaled by one strike of the gavel at the first minute and one strike at the sixth minute).

1.5.3 It is the duty of the Speaker of the House to time speeches.

1.5.4 In the absence of the Speaker of the House, it is the duty of the Chair of the Adjudication panel to ensure that speeches are timed.

1.6 The adjudication

1.6.1 The debate should be adjudicated by a panel of at least three adjudicators, where this is possible.

1.6.2 At the conclusion of the debate, the adjudicators should confer and rank the teams, from first placed to last placed. (see Part 6: The Adjudication).

1.6.3 There will be verbal adjudication of the debate after the first six preliminary rounds of the tournament. The verbal adjudication should be delivered in accordance with clause 6.4 of these rules.

Part 2—Definitions

2.1 The definition

2.1.1 The definition should state the issue (or issues) for debate arising out of the motion and state the meaning of any terms in the motion which require interpretation.

2.1.2 The Prime Minister should provide the definition at the beginning of his or her speech.

2.1.3 The definition must:

(a) have a clear and logical link to the motion—this means that an average reasonable person would accept the link made by the member between the motion and the definition (where there is no such link the definition is sometimes referred to as a "squirrel");

(b) not be self-proving—a definition is self-proving when the case is that something should or should not be done and there is no reasonable rebuttal. A definition may also be self-proving when the case is that a certain state of affairs exists or does not exist and there is no reasonable rebuttal (these definitions are sometimes referred to as "truisms").

(c) not be time set—this means that the debate must take place in the present and that the definition cannot set the debate in the past or the future; and

(d) not be place set unfairly—this means that the definition cannot restrict the debate so narrowly to a particular geographical or political location that a participant of the tournament could not reasonably be expected to have knowledge of the place.

2.2   Challenging the definition

2.2.1 The Leader of the Opposition may challenge the definition if it violates clause 2.1.3 of these rules. The Leader of the Opposition should clearly state that he or she is challenging the definition.

2.2.2 The Leader of the Opposition should substitute an alternative definition after challenging the definition of the Prime Minister.

2.3   Assessing the definitional challenge

2.3.1 The adjudicators should determine the definition to be "unreasonable" where it violates clause 2.1.3 of these rules.

2.3.2 The onus to establish that the definition is unreasonable is on the members asserting that the definition is unreasonable.

2.3.3 Where the definition is unreasonable, the opposition should substitute an alternative definition that should be accepted by the adjudicators provided it is not unreasonable.

2.3.4 Where the definition of the Opening Government is unreasonable and an alternative definition is substituted by the Opening Opposition, the Closing Government may introduce matter which is inconsistent with the matter presented by the Opening Government and consistent with the definition of the Opening Opposition.

2.3.5 If the Opening Opposition has substituted a definition that is also unreasonable, the Closing Government may challenge the definition of the Opening Opposition and substitute an alternative definition.

2.3.6 If the Closing Government has substituted a definition that is also unreasonable (in addition to the unreasonable definitions of the Opening Government and Opening Opposition), the Closing Opposition may challenge the definition of the Closing Government and substitute an alternative definition.

Part 3—Case

3.1 A case, or team line, is a policy, course of action or state of affairs that a team supports and the reasons for which they support it. Opening Government and Opening Opposition should put a case. Closing Government and Closing Opposition should support the same policy, course of action or state of affairs as their opening counterparts but may use different supporting arguments.

Part 4—Matter

4.1 The definition of matter

4.1.1 Matter is the content of the speech. It is the arguments a debater uses to further his or her case and persuade the audience.

4.1.2 Matter includes arguments and reasoning, examples, case studies, facts and any other material that attempts to further the case.

4.1.3 Matter includes positive (or substantive) material and rebuttal (arguments specifically aimed to refute the arguments of the opposing team(s)). Matter includes Points of Information.

4.2   The elements of matter

4.2.1 Matter should be relevant, logical and consistent.

4.2.2 Matter should be relevant. It should relate to the issues of the debate: positive material should support the case being presented and rebuttal should refute the material being presented by the opposing team(s). The Member should appropriately prioritize and apportion time to the dynamic issues of the debate.

4.2.3 Matter should be logical. Arguments should be developed logically in order to be clear and well reasoned and therefore plausible. The conclusion of all arguments should support the Member's case.

4.2.4 Matter should be consistent. Members should ensure that the matter they present is consistent within their speech, their team and the remainder of the members on their side of the debate (subject to clauses 2.3.4, 2.3.5 or 2.3.6 of these rules).

4.2.5 All Members should present positive matter (except the final two Members in the debate) and all Members should present rebuttal (except the first Member in the debate). The Government Whip may choose to present positive matter.

4.2.6 All Members should attempt to answer at least two Points of Information during their own speech and offer Points of Information during opposing speeches.

4.3 Assessing matter

4.3.1 The matter presented should be persuasive. "The elements of matter" should assist an adjudicator to assess the persuasiveness and credibility of the matter presented.

4.3.2 Matter should be assessed from the viewpoint of the average reasonable person. Adjudicators should analyze the matter presented and assess its persuasiveness, while disregarding any specialist knowledge they may have on the issue of the debate.

4.3.3 Adjudicators should not allow bias to influence their assessment. Debaters should not be discriminated against on the basis of religion, sex, race, colour, nationality, sexual preference, age, social status or disability.

4.3.4 Points of Information should be assessed according to the effect they have on the persuasiveness of the cases of both the member answering the Point of Information and the member offering the Point of Information.

Part 5—Manner

5.1 The definition of manner

5.1.1 Manner is the presentation of the speech. It is the style and structure a member uses to further his or her case and persuade the audience.

5.1.2 Manner is composed of many separate elements. Some, but not all, of these elements are listed below.

5.2 The elements of style

5.2.1 The elements of style include eye contact, voice modulation, hand gestures, language, the use of notes and any other element which may affect the effectiveness of the presentation of the member.

5.2.2 Eye contact will generally assist a member to persuade an audience as it allows the member to appear more sincere.

5.2.3 Voice modulation will generally assist a member to persuade an audience as the debater may emphasize important arguments and keep the attention of the audience. This includes the pitch, tone, and volume of the member's voice and the use of pauses.

5.2.4 Hand gestures will generally assist a member to emphasize important arguments. Excessive hand movements may however be distracting and reduce the attentiveness of the audience to the arguments.

5.2.5 Language should be clear and simple. Members who use language which is too verbose or confusing may detract from the argument if they lose the attention of the audience.

5.2.6 The use of notes is permitted, but members should be careful that they do not rely on their notes too much and detract from the other elements of manner.

5.3 The elements of structure

5.3.1 The elements of structure include the structure of the speech of the member and the structure of the speeches of the team.

5.3.2 The matter of the speech of each member must be structured. The member should organize his or her matter to improve the effectiveness of their presentation.

5.3.3 The matter of the team must be structured. The team should organize their matter to improve the effectiveness of their presentation. The team should:

(a) contain a consistent approach to the issues being debated; and

(b) allocate positive matter to each member where both members of the team are introducing positive matter; and

(a) include: an introduction, conclusion and a series of arguments; and

(b) be well-timed in accordance with the time limitations and the need to prioritize and apportion time to matter.

5.4   Assessing manner

5.4.1 Adjudicators should assess the elements of manner together in order to determine the overall effectiveness of the member's presentation. Adjudicators should assess whether the member's presentation is assisted or diminished by their manner.

5.4.2 Adjudicators should be aware that at a World Championship, there are many styles which are appropriate, and that they should not discriminate against a member simply because the manner would be deemed "inappropriate Parliamentary debating" in their own country.

5.4.3 Adjudicators should not allow bias to influence their assessment. Members should not be discriminated against on the basis of religion, sex, race, color, nationality, language (subject to Rule 5.2), sexual preference, age, social status or disability.

Part 6—The Adjudication

6.1   The role of the adjudicator

6.1.1 The adjudicator must:

(a) Confer upon and discuss the debate with the other adjudicators;

(b) Determine the rankings of the teams;

(c) Determine the speaker marks;

(d) Provide a verbal adjudication to the members; and

(e) Complete any documentation required by the tournament.

6.1.2 The adjudication panel should attempt to agree on the adjudication of the debate. Adjudicators should therefore confer in a spirit of cooperation and mutual respect.

6.1.3 Adjudicators should acknowledge that adjudicators on a panel may form different or opposite views of the debate. Adjudicators should therefore attempt to base their conclusions on these rules in order to limit subjectivity and to provide a consistent approach to the assessment of debates.

6.2   Ranking teams

6.2.1 Teams should be ranked from first place to last place. First placed teams should be awarded three points, second placed teams should be awarded two points, third placed teams should be awarded one point and fourth placed teams should be awarded zero points.

6.2.2 Teams may receive zero points where they fail to arrive at the debate more than five minutes after the scheduled time for debate.

6.2.3 Teams may receive zero points where the adjudicators unanimously agree that the Member has (or Members have) harassed another debater on the basis of religion, sex, race, color, nationality, sexual preference or disability.

6.2.4 Adjudicators should confer upon team rankings. Where a unanimous decision cannot be reached after conferral, the decision of the majority will determine the rankings. Where a majority decision cannot be reached, the Chair of the panel of adjudicators will determine the rankings.

6.3   Grading and marking the teams

6.3.1 The panel of adjudicators should agree upon the mark that each individual member is to be awarded.

6.3.2 Individual members' marks should be given the following interpretation:

GRADE	MARK	MEANING
A	90–100	Excellent to flawless. The standard of speech you would expect to see from a speaker at the Semi Final/Grand Final level of the tournament. This speaker has many strengths and few, if any, weaknesses.
B	80–89	Above average to very good. The standard you would expect to see from a speaker at the finals level or in contention to make to the finals. This speaker has clear strengths and some minor weaknesses.
C	70–79	Average. The speaker has strengths and weaknesses in roughly equal proportions.
D	60–69	Poor to below average. The team has clear problems and some minor strengths.
E	50–59	Very poor. This speaker has fundamental weaknesses and few, if any, strengths.

6.3.3 The aggregate of each team's speaker points should correspond to the position of that team in the debate, i.e., the aggregate of the winning team's speaker points must exceed the aggregate of the team coming second, which must exceed the aggregate speaker points of the third-placed team, which must exceed the aggregate speaker points of team placed fourth.

6.4   Verbal adjudications

6.4.1 At the conclusion of the conferral, the adjudication panel should provide a verbal adjudication of the debate.

6.4.2 The verbal adjudication should be delivered by the Chair of the adjudication panel or, where the Chair dissents, by a member of the adjudication panel nominated by the Chair of the panel.

6.4.3 The verbal adjudication should:

(a) identify the order in which the teams were ranked;

(b) explain the reasons for the rankings of team, ensuring that each team is referred to in this explanation; and

(c) provide constructive comments to individual members where the adjudication panel believes this is necessary.

6.4.4 The verbal adjudication should not exceed 10 minutes.

6.4.5 The members must not harass the adjudicators following the verbal adjudication.

6.4.6 The members may approach an adjudicator for further clarification following the verbal adjudication; these inquiries must at all times be polite and non-confrontational.

D

Worlds Hosts and Winners

YEAR	HOSTS	WINNERS
2012	De La Salle, Philippines	
2011	University of Botswana	Monash
2010	Koc, Turkey	Sydney
2009	UCC, Ireland	Oxford
2008	Assumption, Thailand	Oxford
2007	UBC, Canada	Sydney
2006	UCD, Ireland	Toronto
2005	MMU, Malaysia	Ottawa
2004	NTU, Singapore	Middle Temple
2003	Stellenbosch, South Africa	Cambridge
2002	Toronto, Canada	New York
2001	Glasgow, Scotland	Sydney
2000	Sydney, Australia	Monash
1999	Ateneo de Manila, Philippines	Monash
1998	Deree College, Greece	Grays Inn
1997	Stellenbosch, South Africa	Glasgow
1996	UCC, Ireland	Macquarie
1995	Princeton, USA	UNSW

YEAR	HOSTS	WINNERS
1994	Melbourne, Australia	Glasgow
1993	Oxford, England	Harvard
1992	TCD, Ireland	Glasgow
1991	Toronto, Canada	McGill
1990	Glasgow, Scotland	Yale
1989	Princeton, USA	Sydney
1988	Sydney, Australia	Oxford
1987	UCD, Ireland	Glasgow
1986	Fordham, USA	UCC
1985	McGill, Canada	King's Inns
1984	Edinburgh, Scotland	Sydney
1983	Princeton, USA	Glasgow
1982	Toronto, Canada	Auckland
1981	Glasgow, Scotland	Toronto

Glossary

Terms you need to understand,
words debaters like to say.

Adjudication Panel the people who judge a debate.

Adjudicator a person who judges a debate.

Analysis the process of developing an argument, introducing and assessing evidence. Adjudicators often ask for more analysis.

Analysis debate a debate that asks what the world is like, rather than what should be done about it.

Argument a point made logically.

Audience people listening to a debate.

Back-tabbing a process by which debaters try to work out the results during closed adjudication rounds.

Ballot the formal record of results in each room.

Bottom half Closing Government and Closing Opposition.

Break (n.) the point at which the elimination rounds are announced; (v.) to progress to the elimination rounds.

Breaking on speaks progressing to the elimination rounds on the basis of speaker points, having achieved the same team points as one or more teams that failed to progress.

Break rounds *See* Elimination rounds

Bubble round one of the debates, in the final preliminary round of a competition, in which one or more teams has an arithmetical chance of breaking.

Case a policy, course of action, or state of affairs supported by a team and the reasons for which they support it.

Casefile a file containing notes, articles, and information compiled by a debater to help her or him prepare for debates.

Chair the presiding adjudicator who chairs the adjudication panel and holds the casting vote in the event of a tie.

Challenge a formal challenge to the current definition; it seeks to replace current definition with another.

Chief Adjudicator (CA) the person responsible for overseeing the organization of debates at a tournament.

Circular argument an argument that assumes what it is trying to prove.

Clash the points of disagreement in a debate.

Closed adjudication the situation where results and feedback cannot be given to teams by adjudicators after their debate.

Closing half collectively, the Closing Government and Closing Opposition teams.

Constructive (n.) arguments, as opposed to rebuttal.

Contradiction an inconsistency between two arguments.

Core Adjudication Team together, the Chief Adjudicator and Deputy Chief Adjudicators.

Counteropp a case, made by Opening Opposition, that posits a specific alternative course of action to that proposed by Opening Government.

Definition the policy, course of action, or state of affairs supported by the Opening Government team.

Deputy Chief Adjudicator (DCA) person appointed to help the Chief Adjudicator oversee the organization of debates at a tournament.

Deputy Leader of the Opposition second speaker on the Opposition.

Deputy Prime Minister second speaker on the Government.

Dichotomy division of something into two discrete parts, but used by some debaters to mean "contradiction."

Draw assignment of specific teams to debates.

Dummy team see Swing team.

EFL English as a foreign language.

Engagement showing points of agreement and disagreement with other teams in the debate.

Elimination rounds the octofinals, quarterfinals, semifinals, and final.

Equity Officer person responsible for ensuring fair treatment of participants at a tournament.

ESL English as a second language.

ESL break the break open to ESL teams.

EUDC European Universities Debating Championships.

Euros the European Universities Debating Championships, also known as EUDC.

Extension a new argument or arguments.

Floor debate debate between audience members continued after the main debate and before the result is announced.

Framing using labels and vocabulary that are helpful to your side.

Gov Government.

Government the side in favor of the motion.

Government Whip fourth speaker on the Government.

Harm results that would occur if the issue being debated were not solved. Debaters are often eager to prove the presence or absence of harm to others, usually invoking J. S. Mill's famous principle from *On Liberty*, to establish whether a course of action is justified.

Intervarsity competition tournament between teams from different universities.

Iron man (v.) to speak in two positions, thus replacing a whole team, in order to make up the numbers at a competition where a swing team is not available.

IV intervarsity competition.

Knife (n.) statement that contradicts a definition, case, or argument previously accepted by that side, team, or speaker; (v.) to utter such a statement.

Knockout rounds *See* Elimination rounds.

Ladies and Gentlemen traditional opening for a speech, sometimes used as a time filler by debaters.

Leader of the Opposition first speaker on the Opposition.

Long diagonal Opening Government and Closing Opposition. Used by some adjudicators when referring to the interaction between these two teams.

Main break (where a tournament has ESL and/or EFL categories) the teams progressing from the preliminary rounds to the (non-ESL and/or non-EFL) elimination rounds.

Manner presentation of a speech, including its style and structure.

Matter content of a speech, including Points of Information.

Mechanism account of how the definition will be implemented.

Member of the Government third speaker on the Government.

Member of the Opposition third speaker on the Opposition.

Minus 1, 2, 3, etc. expression of the degree by which the number of team points possessed by a team falls short of the number obtained by a hypothetical team finishing second in every round to date.

Model definition.

Motion the topic for debate, worded "This House ..."

Negative externality a cost imposed on others.

Open a tournament open to all.

Open adjudication the situation where results and feedback can be given to teams by adjudicators after the debate.

Opening half collectively, the Opening Government and Opening Opposition teams.

Open motion motion that allows Opening Government to introduce a topic of their choice for debate.

Opp abbreviation of Opposition.

Opposition the side against the motion.

Opposition Whip fourth speaker on the Opposition.

Oral adjudication see Verbal adjudication.

Othering currently fashionable term used by debaters to describe division into "them" and "us,"

Panacea originally the Greek goddess of healing, often used to characterize a case as unrealistic.

Plan definition.

Platform debate where there is a floor debate involving members of the audience, the term *platform debate* can be used to denote the main debate (which comes before it).

Plus 1, 2, 3, etc. expression of the degree by which the number of team points possessed by a team surpasses the number obtained by a hypothetical team finishing second in every round to date.

POI Point of Information.

Point of Information (POI) brief comment or question put to a speaker on the opposing side to which they must respond directly.

Positive externality a benefit conferred on others.

Positive matter new arguments.

Prep or prep time the period (usually 15 minutes) between the announcement of the motion and the start of the debate; used by teams to prepare.

Prime Minister first speaker on the Government.

Prop (1) an abbreviation of Proposition, an alternative term for Government; (2) an abbreviation of proposal, meaning definition.

Proposal an alternative word for definition; the policy, course of action, or state of affairs supported by Opening Government.

Proposition an alternative word for Government.

Rebuttal arguments that counter those previously made by the other side.

Role individual or team position in the debate.

Roll (v.) for the wing judges to outvote the Chair.

Seconds number of team points equivalent to those gained by a hypothetical team finishing second in every round to date.

Self-actualization term frequently used by debaters meaning the realization of one's potential.

Short diagonal Opening Opposition and Closing Government. Used by some adjudicators when referring to the interaction between these two teams.

Side every debate has two sides: Government and Opposition.

Side Government the Government.

Side Opposition the Opposition.

Signposting telling people what you (and your partner) are going to say.

Social utility a term preferred by some debaters to "affecting other people."

Speaker (a) person responsible for keeping order in a public debate; (b) the debater speaking.

Speaker tab league table showing the rank order of speakers based on individual points.

Split division of points between two speakers on a team.

Squirrel a definition with no clear and logical link to the motion.

Status quo the current state of affairs. The phrase "in the status quo" is often preferred by debaters to the word *now*.

Straw man a weakened version of an argument, expressed by a speaker in an attempt to make rebuttal easier. Not recommended.

Structure organization of the content of a speech to aid the effectiveness of presentation.

Style eye contact, voice modulation, hand gestures, language, the use of notes, and anything else that affects effective presentation.

Substantive new arguments.

Substantive case new arguments.

Swing team team of debaters formed to make up the numbers at a tournament; this team cannot break to the elimination rounds.

Sweep where first and second place are awarded to teams on the same side of the table—called a "prop sweep" or "opp sweep" as appropriate.

Tab formal record of results across a tournament.

Tangible a word favored by debaters over *harm* and *benefits*; it is used for emphasis.

Team line case.

Team tab league table showing the ranking of teams.

Timekeeper person, usually a wing, responsible for keeping time and signaling both protected time and the end of each speech.

Tournament director person responsible for running the tab at a competition.

Top half Opening Government and Opening Opposition.

Trainee an adjudicator who plays no part in the adjudication panel but learns from witnessing its operation.

Utopian a word, derived from Sir Thomas More's novel, used by debaters to dismiss a case as unrealistic.

Verbal adjudication formal session after a debate where the Chair gives the result and feedback to teams.

Wing adjudicator who is not the Chair.

WODC World Online Debating Championships.

Worlds World Universities Debating Championships.

WUDC World Universities Debating Championships.